sew cool
sew simple

Stylish Skirts

sew cool
sew simple

Stylish Skirts

Valerie Van Arsdale Shrader

LARK BOOKS

A Division of Sterling Publishing Co., Inc.
New York

ART DIRECTOR & ILLUSTRATOR:
Susan McBride

COVER DESIGNER:
Barbara Zaretsky

ASSOCIATE EDITOR:
Nathalie Mornu

ASSISTANT EDITOR:
Rebecca Guthrie

ASSOCIATE ART DIRECTOR:
Shannon Yokeley

ART PRODUCTION ASSISTANT:
Jeff Hamilton

EDITORIAL ASSISTANCE:
Dawn Dillingham,
Delores Gosnell

PHOTOGRAPHER:
Stewart O'Shields

ART INTERN:
Ardyce E. Alspach

EDITORIAL INTERNS:
David L. Squires,
Sue Stigleman

Library of Congress Cataloging-in-Publication Data

Shrader, Valerie Van Arsdale.
  Sew cool, sew simple : stylish skirts / Valerie Van Arsdale Shrader.-- 1st
ed.
      p. cm.
  Includes index.
  ISBN 1-57990-724-5 (hardcover)
  1. Skirts. 2. Sewing. I. Title.
TT540.S37 2006
646.4'37--dc22

                                              2005030467

10 9 8 7 6 5 4 3 2 1

First Edition

Published by Lark Books, A Division of
Sterling Publishing Co., Inc.
387 Park Avenue South, New York, N.Y. 10016

© 2006, Lark Books

Distributed in Canada by Sterling Publishing,
c/o Canadian Manda Group, 165 Dufferin Street
Toronto, Ontario, Canada M6K 3H6

Distributed in the United Kingdom by GMC Distribution Services,
Castle Place, 166 High Street, Lewes, East Sussex, England BN7 1XU

Distributed in Australia by Capricorn Link (Australia) Pty Ltd.,
P.O. Box 704, Windsor, NSW 2756 Australia

If you have questions or comments about this book,
please contact:
Lark Books
67 Broadway
Asheville, NC 28801
(828) 253-0467

Manufactured in China

ISBN 13: 978-1-57990-724-2
ISBN 10: 1-57990-724-5

For information about custom editions, special sales, premium and corporate
purchases, please contact Sterling Special Sales Department at 800-805-5489
or specialsales@sterlingpub.com.

You're going to like what you see in this book!

Contents

Embellishment Techniques 100

Introduction

Could you possibly be suffering from skirt envy? I certainly used to. Here are a few of the symptoms: heart palpitations at the sight of the latest hemline or glorious embellishment; uncontrollable sighing over the luxurious feel of a silken hem; utter disappointment when the right size or color isn't available; or complete shock at the purchase price.

Fear not, my friends, for I have cured myself of skirt envy, and I can cure you, too. How, you might ask? Why, by inspiring you to make your own fabulous skirts! When you see the to-die-for skirts in this book, you'll rush right for the sewing machine. A skirt is the perfect project because it's quick to make, uses relatively little fabric, and can be easily embellished for a unique fashion statement. Even with an indulgence in expensive fabric, your skirt is bound to be cheaper than paying boutique prices. And there's no distress when your size can't be found on the rack.

Well, why the sad face then? Oh, I see—you really don't know *how* to sew. Let me guess why. Your middle school attempt was a disaster. Your home ec teacher was an uptight … perfectionist— and you weren't. The sewing

We love our skirts!

machine was confusing. The pink culottes you had to make were scary. Having to wear them to school was even *scarier*. The entire experience just wasn't hip.

As you're probably aware, times have changed and so has garment construction. Check out the skirts in stores or in catalogs and look at the deconstructed details—an exposed seam with raw edges, an unfinished hem, a raggedy line of zigzag stitching, or gloriously mismatched fabrics stitched together in perfect harmony. While the techniques haven't changed much, the way they are used and the attitudes toward them have. Before the Age of Enlightenment, we had to hide all the raw edges inside a skirt, but sewers are now free to leave an edge unfinished on the outside (gasp!)

to let the fabric happily ravel. Or to use orange trim on a red skirt or not even use a facing on the waist. Your home ec teacher is probably having a fit right now; what in the world has happened to sewing? Well, this is what has happened: sewing has been liberated from the home ec teachers of the world and handed right back to us creative geniuses where it belongs. Sewing, in case you haven't noticed, is now *cool*.

And what a coincidence … skirts are cool, too. They're long, short, full, slim, embellished, gathered, tiered—if you can dream it, you can make it. *Stylish Skirts* will take you through the entire process, from selecting patterns and fabric to sewing and embellishing. But you won't be overwhelmed with information, because we'll focus on making skirts and not one thing more. After we talk about some basic skills, you'll see how easy it is to plan, make, and decorate your own skirts. The 10 skirts included here offer a wide range of styles, techniques, and fabrics … think of them as the hip home ec experience you never had. And guess what? In the process of making skirts, you'll acquire the handy skill of sewing.

Best of all, you'll never—*ever*—suffer from skirt envy again.

An exposed raw edge? What would your home ec teacher think?

9

Guide to
Stylish Skirt Making

Lovely design, fun fabric, and champagne, too!

When you're afflicted by skirt envy, what happens? You're attracted to the style, of course, so the skirt's appearance has to please you. When you touch the fabric, you can't wait to put it on. These two elements, the design and the fabric, are the key to making a skirt you'll love. Deciding which comes first—the fabric or the pattern—depends on your mindset. But since this book is all about stylish skirts, let's start with the pattern, the actual design you'll use to make your first skirt.

If you're new to sewing (remember, you've got to learn how if you want to make a skirt), it helps to understand the information in a pattern and how the kind of skirt you want to make will be affected by your fabric choice. You become the designer and the creator of your wardrobe when you sew, so there's more freedom than you have when you shop for a skirt—no more liking the style, but settling for a so-so color. Now *you* choose which patterns to use, which details to include, and which fabric to splurge on. You're no longer at the mercy of ready-to-wear and you can really apply your personality to your wardrobe.

Since I'm a fabric junkie and an experienced sewer, I tend to be attracted to fabrics first and then find a pattern. But I think it helps the new (or reincarnated) sewer to understand patterns first, and then choose the right fabric. So let's first talk about patterns, and then fabric. We'll deal with that sewing stuff later (after a nice cup of chai), when we go through the process of making a skirt in detail. I promise not to overload you with information about sewing that you don't need and probably won't ever use; we're trying to keep it as simple as we can. Finally, we'll get right down to it and make 10 fab skirts. All the information you'll find in this section of the book will be a foundation for the actual projects themselves, so refer to it as often as you need to.

Pick a pattern

You'll be pleased and probably relieved to know that a skirt doesn't have to be difficult to be the perfect expression of you. In *Stylish Skirts*, you'll learn all the steps to create beautiful skirts—but it's okay, we won't tackle everything at once. Each of the 10 projects in the book offers skills in a progressive manner, so you can create an entire wardrobe of skirts and expand your repertoire of skills with each project. The patterns we've chosen use basic techniques, but also add some contemporary details such as ribbon embellishments, deconstructed seams, unfinished hems, and creative stitching. Patterns (and all that stuff inside) sometimes seem intimidating, but actually the pattern is the key to the skirt of your dreams. Let's talk about patterns in general terms now; we'll find out how to actually use them when we Learn to Sew! on page 25.

Trying to decide between patterns? Look for details you want to include in your skirt, such as pleats or gathers.

Fabric shops offer a variety of catalogs from the major pattern companies. Each company issues a new catalog seasonally, just as designers continually produce new collections, so you can be sure to find current designs as well as classic silhouettes. The pattern catalogs are like Fashion Week in a book! When you visit your local fabric shop, look through the skirt sections of the various catalogs for all the possibilities. When you find a style that appeals to you, read through the information about the skirt. Generally, you'll find out how much fabric you need, what type of fabric is recommended for that style, and which other notions (zippers, buttons, etc.) you'll need to make the skirt. Most patterns offer variations on the basic design, sometimes as many as six in one envelope. (More for your money!) The variations are usually labeled with letters (View A, Skirt B, etc.).

or ?

A typical pattern envelope

STYLE, FIT, AND CONSTRUCTION DETAILS.
This describes the kind of skirt you'll be making.

PATTERN NAME AND NUMBER.
Here's the skirt you found in the pattern catalog.

SKIRT

FABRIC

NOTIONS

easy   facile

B4522

FABRIC SUGGESTIONS.
Choose from this list of suggested fabrics.

NOTIONS. In addition to the pattern and the fabric, here's the other stuff you'll need to make your skirt.

FABRIC REQUIREMENTS.
Follow the columns below your size to find out how much fabric you need.

A   B   C   D   E

VARIATIONS. Here are all the cute skirts you can make from this pattern.

This side is usually in French. Trés chic, non?

FINISHED MEASUREMENTS.
Some of the measurements for the finished skirt will be listed on the pattern envelope.

12

Outside the pattern envelope

Now, after you find an irresistible design in the catalog, study the pattern envelope itself for even more information. Practically every pattern used in this book was labeled "Easy" or "Fast" or something similar. Until you've gained some skills and confidence (which won't be long), stick to patterns that are similarly labeled. Refer to the illustration on the opposite page as we talk about what you'll learn from the pattern envelope.

STYLE, FIT, AND CONSTRUCTION DETAILS. It may say something like, "Loose-fitting pull-on skirt in two lengths and bias skirt in three lengths," or "A-line, below mid-knee length skirt has asymmetrical hemline and side zipper." This listing gives you specific information about the style of the skirt and its construction.

You should also know about *ease*. Patterns include varying amounts of wearing ease and design ease. Wearing ease is the additional sizing included in your skirt so you can move in it, while design ease is added to achieve a particular silhouette. The terms you see on your pattern envelope, such as "loose-fitting" or "fitted," refer to design ease. The amount of ease you prefer is personal, so if you like things close-fitting, don't buy a pattern for a loose-fitting garment.

NOTIONS. Patterns list all the additional items that you need to finish the project, such as "1 yard of ½-inch elastic" or "7-inch zipper, 3 yards of ¾-inch-wide ribbon trim."

FABRIC SUGGESTIONS. Most companies list a range of fabrics that will be suitable for the skirt designs, including things like "silks and silk types, cotton and cotton blends, and lightweight denim." We'll spend more time talking about fabric in just a few minutes, but the important thing to understand now is that you'll have lots of appropriate fabric choices for each design.

FABRIC REQUIREMENTS. You'll find out how much fabric you need to make your chosen skirt.

FINISHED MEASUREMENTS. The extent of this information varies among pattern companies, but generally you'll find the hip

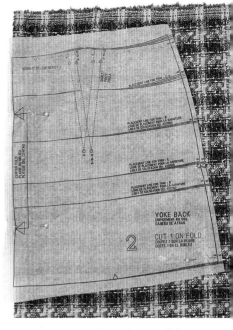

The pattern pieces themselves are full of information.

measurements, length, and width of the finished skirt. Note that the hip measurements will differ from actual body measurements because they include ease, as we just discussed.

Inside the pattern envelope

The envelope contains the pattern pieces themselves, printed on tissue paper, and the instructions for the skirt. Don't be overwhelmed by the information inside, because it's all presented in small digestible bits. We should be thankful that the pattern companies have figured out how to give us so much useful stuff in such a tidy package.

PATTERN PIECES. Modern patterns generally contain more than one size, and all the pieces for the skirt will be printed on one or more large sheets of tissue paper. When you've identified your size and the style you want to make (Skirt B, let's say), refer to the instruction sheet for a key to tell you which pieces you need to use.

INSTRUCTIONS. You'll find cutting layouts, which illustrate how to place the pattern pieces on the fabric and cut them out. You'll also have sewing directions, which give you step-by-step instructions on making your skirt. There are also some general sewing tips to supplement the instructions; we're going to cover all this basic information here, too. Read over the instructions completely before you begin making your skirt so you understand the sequence of its construction. *Please*.

Which size?

You probably won't admit it, but I bet this is the real reason you've avoided learning to sew. Pattern companies don't use the same sizing that apparel manufacturers use. Take a deep breath before I tell you that you may need to buy a pattern that's two, three, or possibly *four* sizes larger than what you'd buy in ready-to-wear. I hear you moaning now, but think through this logically; it's just a number, after all. The system of sizing the pattern companies use is simply different.

To demonstrate this, here's a comparison of measurements:

	MAJOR PATTERN COMPANY	MAJOR APPAREL COMPANY
Bust	32½	32½
Waist	25	25
Hip	34½	35
Size	**10**	**2**

Amazing, isn't it? This, my dear, is a practice called *vanity sizing*: the garment industry cuts its clothing generously while putting a teeny little size on the tag. Neither be fooled nor disappointed by this trickery.

To make sure your skirt fits, measure yourself accurately according to the illustration on the next page. Buy the size that most closely matches your hip measurement. Measure your hips approximately nine inches below your waist or at the spot where your hips are the widest. Now, forget about the garment industry—you're making your own skirts now.

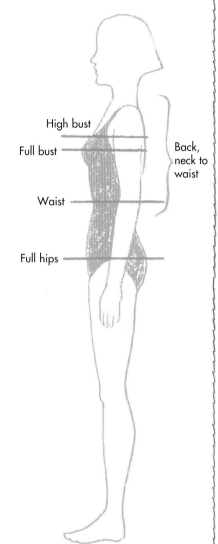

High bust

Full bust

Back, neck to waist

Waist

Full hips

Choose your fabric

Okay, you've found a pattern for a great skirt. You love it! Now the search for fabric begins. This is the exciting part of making a skirt, because your project starts to breathe when you can feel the fabric. Imagine that you're in Paris and you could have any skirt you wanted; making your own skirt is absolutely no different, because you *can* have anything you want. Spend some quality time looking for fabric. If you don't like the color, or the print, or the drape of the fabric, you won't like the skirt. Remember that your pattern envelope will offer you a variety of fabrics that are suitable for your skirt, so be sure to choose one of the types that's suggested.

These are swatches of fabrics used in the Make A Skirt! section. All are cotton, except for the orange print, which is a vintage synthetic crepe.

Fabric basics

I won't bore you with lots of information about fabric, because I suspect you'll become entranced with it and learn a lot on your own. (I've already cast the spell.) But a little general information is definitely in order. Fabrics are made of fibers of various origins. Since you're into clothes, you probably already have a basic knowledge of the different types of fabric and what they are made from: the natural fibers, such as cotton, linen, wool, and silk; and the synthetic fibers, like polyester, acrylic, and nylon. (Thank you, chemists!) Rayon straddles these two categories, as it's synthesized from wood pulp; it's manmade, yet from a natural source.

15

Other synthetic fabrics are made from sources such as petroleum products, and many fabrics are blends of natural *and* synthetic fibers.

The weave of the fabric gives it certain characteristics. Satin, velvet, twill, and so on all describe the structure of the fabric, and not its fiber content. Velvet can be made from silk, cotton, or polyester, for example. But when you're learning to make a skirt, the properties of the fabric (drape, texture, weight, etc.) are just as important as the fiber content. As long as it hangs the way it's supposed to, you have some flexibility as to what you can use. These are the parameters the pattern companies use when they suggest a range of fabrics for a specific design. Isn't that thoughtful of them? I think so.

The right fabric is the key to loving your skirt. Here are more swatches from our skirts. From left to right: silk chiffon; a linen/rayon blend; a fine cotton; and an embroidered linen/rayon blend.

Here are two interesting fabrics we used in this book. The bouclé tweed has a little sparkle from a metallic thread, and the black cotton eyelet has heavenly embroidery.

Will it work?

So how do you know whether your fabric will drape properly? Well, you can tell a lot from fabric by touching and manipulating it before you buy it. (Don't worry. The folks in the fabric stores are used to people fondling fabric.) In all seriousness, you really must feel the material, as you'll be working with it and wearing it—is it smooth? Thin or heavy? Stiff or soft? Unfold a length of fabric from the bolt and observe how it hangs. If you want a skirt with a little flounce that drapes just so, you need a lightweight fabric; if you want a crisp silhouette, a medium-weight linen might be just perfect.

Each bolt of fabric will be labeled with its fiber content, its width, its price, and occasionally its laundering requirements. Be sure to ask about laundering the fabric

A totally cool fabric +
a simple pattern =
a great skirt.

Simply put, don't use a fabric that feels slippery for your first skirt, because it's likely to scoot around when you cut it or sew with it, and you're likely to get discouraged. A common mistake that beginners make is choosing a luscious fabric that requires some experience to properly handle. Believe me when I tell you that there are beautiful cottons available that will make your first skirt a happy experience.

before you buy it, so you understand how to care for your skirt after you've made it. Washable fabrics need to be preshrunk before being sewn, which simply means laundering them according to the manufacturer's recommendations before you start.

For a first skirt, I suggest a medium-weight cotton, because it handles well, it's durable, it's easy to sew, and it washes well. Most of the skirt projects in this book are made from cotton, linen, rayon, or blends of those fibers. (All of these are woven fabrics; there are no knits used in *Stylish Skirts*.) While slinky charmeuse or flimsy chiffon might be beautiful, they're a little more difficult to handle than the fabrics listed above and thus not well suited for a first skirt project. (Now, a second or third project? That's a different story.)

With fabric like this, you'll want to sew all day!

Meet the Sewing Machine

The next step is to develop a meaningful relationship with your sewing machine, since it's the tool that will free you from skirt envy. Give it a friendly little pat and let's get to know it better. Later, when we Learn to Sew! on page 25, we'll discuss some of its functions in greater detail. I *love* my sewing machine! I really do.

How it works

This fantastic invention creates a lockstitch when the thread from the needle (on top of the machine) and the thread from the bobbin (inside the machine) loop together in the fabric. This happens a gazillion times per minute when you sew. (Aren't you glad you don't have to do it by hand? I sure am.) That's the long, the short, and the zigzag of it.

Although machines share common characteristics, they vary by manufacturer. When I keep referring you to your own machine's manual, I'm not trying to ignore your needs; it's because there are some important yet subtle differences between machines that might confuse you. For instance, the thread on my machine disappears inside for part of its journey—yours might not. My bobbin winds on the front of the machine—yours might be on top. I have a pressure foot dial, but you might have a lever. Despite that rambling disclaimer, let's have a go at some general information anyway.

See the illustration on the opposite page: a typical machine has a spool (or spools) for the thread; controls for stitch width, stitch length, thread tension, and presser foot pressure (say that three times fast); a handwheel; a take-up lever; tension disks; a presser foot lever; thread guides; a bobbin winder; a needle; a presser foot; feed dogs; a needle plate; and a bobbin. All of these things furiously work together to create the little lockstitch that makes the skirt that cures skirt envy.

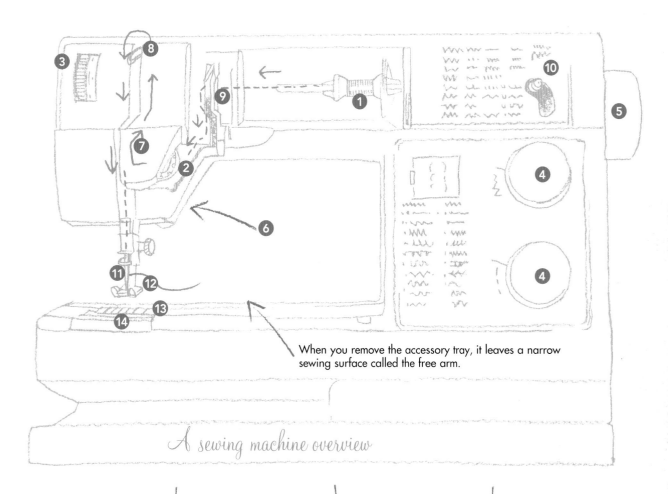

When you remove the accessory tray, it leaves a narrow sewing surface called the free arm.

A sewing machine overview

1. The spool holds the thread.

2. This dial adjusts the thread tension; turn it in tiny increments.

3. Adjust the pressure of the presser foot with this dial.

4. These dials adjust stitch selection, including width and length.

5. The handwheel revolves when you sew, and you can turn it by hand for precision work.

6. The presser foot lever (hiding in the back) lifts the presser foot and engages the tension disks. Remember to put it in the down position when you sew! But lift the presser foot when you thread your machine.

7. The tension disks, tucked inside the machine, regulate the movement of the thread.

8. The take-up lever carries the thread while the machine is sewing, pulling the exact amount it needs for each stitch. If this lever isn't threaded properly, an unsightly gob of thread will appear on your fabric.

9. The thread guides move the thread through the machine in an orderly fashion.

10. The bobbin winder winds the thread on the bobbin. (It's not named very creatively, is it?)

11. The needle pierces the fabric and creates a stitch when it's looped together with the thread from the bobbin. Use the right size needle for your fabric, and use a new needle for each project.

12. The presser foot keeps the fabric snug against the feed dogs, the little serrated thingies that move the fabric as you sew.

13. The needle plate is the metal surface through which the needle grabs the bobbin thread. It has handy guidelines for seam allowances.

14. The bobbin is wound with thread and lives inside the machine. The looping of the thread from the spool with the thread from the bobbin forms the basic lockstitch.

Most modern machines have a detachable accessory tray that's part of the sewing surface; when it's removed, a narrow sewing surface called a *free arm* remains. The free arm lets you stitch around narrow openings like sleeves.

In case you could have possibly forgotten (!), your sewing machine manual is the best source of information for your particular model. It will have detailed information about threading the machine; winding the bobbin; adjusting stitch width and length; and selecting any specialty stitches. Read through the manual thoroughly before you begin to make your skirt and practice stitching to familiarize yourself with the operation of your machine. It will be fun!

Use the right needle

There's no great mystery to choosing the proper needle for your skirt. The three major types are sharps, for use on finely woven fabrics; ballpoints, for knits; and universal points, for all-purpose sewing on both knits and woven fabrics. Needles come in different sizes, with the smaller numbers for use on lightweight fabrics and the larger numbers for heavyweight material. They are marked in both European (60, 70, etc.) and American (10, 12, and so on) sizes; which number comes first depends on the manufacturer. A universal point in the medium range (70/10 or 80/12, for instance) will suit most of the fabric used in this book. For the easy way out, try this: when you buy your fabric, smile brightly at the clerk and ask for a recommendation.

Use the right presser foot

The presser foot is the gismo that keeps the fabric secure against the feed dogs; the feed dogs are the gismos that move the fabric along as you sew. There are lots of specialized presser feet designed to perform specific tasks, but we keep it simple in this book by only using two: a general presser foot that allows both straight and zigzag stitching, and the zipper foot, which lets you stitch close to the zipper when you're installing it. That handy manual of yours will instruct you on changing the presser feet.

Got Sewing Machine?

If you already have a sewing machine, you're ready to make a skirt. But, please hear this: The machine is really, really important, because if it doesn't operate properly, you won't be able to sew successfully. And you won't make any stylish skirts.

If you don't have a sewing machine, here are a few things to consider when buying or borrowing one.

1 You don't have to spend a ton of money to get a perfectly good entry-level sewing machine. But you really should go to a dealer and test-drive before you buy. Sew over different thicknesses of fabric, thread it yourself, wind the bobbin, check out the stitch selection, make a buttonhole—dealers expect and welcome this level of scrutiny from their customers. Many dealers offer an introductory class after you've purchased a machine.

2 If you buy a used machine, insist on that test-drive, too. Stitching can look dreadfully wonky when there's actually not much wrong (maybe just a tension adjustment on the bobbin), but then again, maybe that poor machine has been abused. Have a reputable dealer inspect it before you plunk down your hard-earned cash. Make sure that you have a complete operating manual, too.

3 If you borrow a machine, please don't make the mistake of hauling a dusty machine out of someone's attic and thinking it will sew beautifully. Maybe it will, but probably it won't; sewing machines need to be tuned up regularly, just like cars. They work awfully hard, and they accumulate lots of dust from fabric and thread. (This dust migrates into the screwiest places, too.) Get a proper introduction from the machine's owner (do a lot of the same things I suggest when you're shopping for a machine) and have the owner point out its important features. Don't forget to borrow that manual, also. (As if!)

Gather the Tools and Supplies

In addition to the sewing machine, you need to gather up a few other tools and materials before you begin your first skirt. All of these items are readily available at any fabric shop.

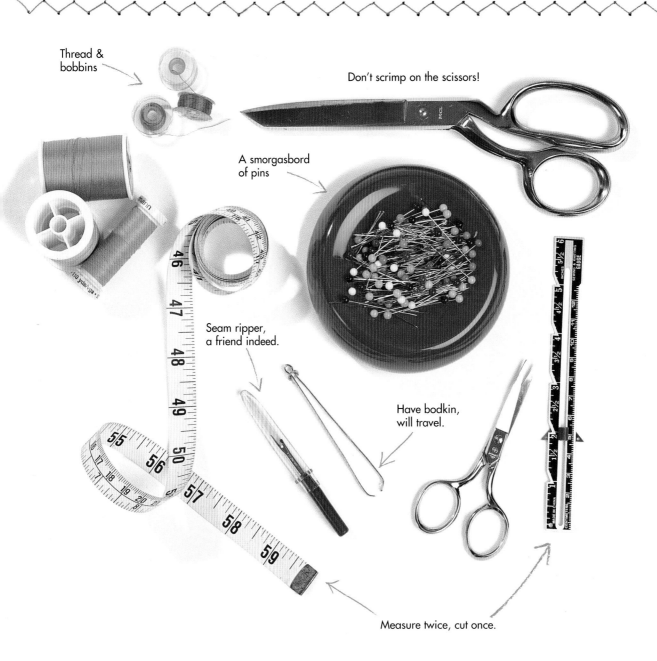

Thread & bobbins

Don't scrimp on the scissors!

A smorgasbord of pins

Seam ripper, a friend indeed.

Have bodkin, will travel.

Measure twice, cut once.

SCISSORS. If you invest in only one quality item for making skirts, I suggest a good pair of 7- or 8-inch dressmaker's bent-handled shears. The design of bent-handled shears allows the fabric to remain flat, so it doesn't shift while you're cutting. A pair of sewing scissors, say 4 to 5 inches long, is perfect for other cutting tasks, such as trimming seams. Buy the best scissors you can afford, because they'll be your friend forever. I still use my grandmother's sewing scissors, which are at least 30 (if not 40) years old.

Though you should use dressmaker's shears to cut out your skirt, a pair of pinking shears is handy to finish seams. And they're cute, too.

SEAM RIPPER. Change is inevitable, and so are mistakes. Use a seam ripper to remove stitches that displease you.

MEASURING TOOLS. If the only measuring tool you had were a tape measure, you could certainly make a skirt. But a couple of other gadgets will be useful, too: a clear ruler helps while cutting out fabric, and a sewing gauge is a nifty little tool that has a slider for marking lengths. I find that I rely on my sewing gauge quite often—for marking hems, placing trim, and all types of petite measuring tasks.

PINS & NEEDLES. Basic dressmaker's pins will be fine for your early skirt projects. Later on, you may want to add thin silk pins or long quilter's pins (with adorable colorful heads) to your stash of sewing supplies.

You'll do very little hand sewing for the projects in this book. An assortment of sharps (all-purpose sewing needles) is fine.

PINCUSHION. Store all of your pins and needles in a pincushion. You can get the ubiquitous tomato or the groovy felt orb, or perhaps try a magnetic pin-cushion. Lately I've come to favor the magnetic variety because they can grab the pins that have misbehaved and escaped to the floor.

THREAD. All-purpose thread, which is cotton-wrapped polyester, is fine for any of the skirts in this book. As your adventure in sewing continues, you may eventually want to use all-cotton thread (great for woven, natural fiber fabrics) or perhaps all-polyester thread (good for fiber blends and knits). When you're choosing a thread color for your skirt, either match it to the fabric or choose a shade that's slightly darker.

BODKIN. Sounds like something from Tolkien, doesn't it? Actually, a bodkin is an ingenious tool used to thread elastic through the casing of our pull-on skirts. You'll see one of these in action on page 54. (For the thrifty, a big safety pin is a good alternative to using a bodkin;

just pin it to the end of the elastic and feed it through the casing.)

MARKING TOOLS. Your pattern pieces will have some markings (circles, center points, darts, and the like) that need to be transferred to the fabric. There are several different ways you can accomplish this: with tailor's chalk or chalk pencil, with water-soluble or air-soluble (i.e. disappearing) fabric pens, or with tracing paper and a tracing wheel. You should always test your marking supplies on a scrap of fabric before you begin your skirt. We'll take some of these tools for a spin when we put them to use on page 29.

MISCELLANEOUS NOTIONS. In case you're interested, notions include all the other things you need to sew besides the pattern and fabric. We've already talked about the most important things you'll need, but here's a quick word about a few other items.

The skirt projects begin with a couple of simple pull-on skirts, so you'll need some elastic for the waist. Then we use

Marking tools

zippers. Many of the skirts have *interfacing* at the waist; interfacing is special fabric that's used to stabilize areas in your skirt. All of the skirts in this book use fusible interfacing that bonds to the fabric with heat and pressure. Some of the skirts also include narrow twill tape, which is applied to the waistline to prevent it from stretching.

IRON. You can't make a skirt without an iron; pressing is very important to set seams and to the success of your final product. Note that we're not talking about *ironing*, which is sliding your iron across the fabric. We're talking about *pressing*. Pressing is moving the iron across the fabric in increments by pressing it up and down. Press open each seam before it's overlapped or crossed by another seam. Remember—up and down, not side to side. Ironing can distort the grain of your fabric.

Learn to Sew!

Without further ado, or even a drumroll, let's begin to make a skirt. If the process of sewing has intimidated you before, maybe you ought to think about it as you would the process of cooking. You choose a recipe (the pattern); buy the ingredients (fabric and notions); do the washing and chopping (preparing and cutting out the fabric); and then add the ingredients to one another according to the recipe (sew by following the pattern instructions.) See—easy as pie. Or, if you'd rather—a piece of cake!

Back to the topic at hand.
Let's begin with the fabric.

Prepare the fabric

You have to know a little more about fabric to understand the importance of the proper layout and subsequent cutting of your skirt, so bear with me a moment. When we discussed fabric earlier, we talked about prewashing. Now, prewashing actually means *shrinking*, as many washable fabrics will do just that when laundered. Generally, the looser the weave, the more shrinkage is likely to occur. Washing also removes sizing or finishes that may affect your stitches. Check the label on the bolt of cloth for the laundering recommendations, and launder the fabric the same way you plan to launder the skirt. Please don't neglect this very important step, because you'll be totally bummed to wash your skirt for the first time and then find that it's way too small for you. After you've laundered your fabric, press it to remove any wrinkles.

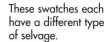

These swatches each have a different type of selvage.

Align the grain

Your fabric must be correctly aligned before you cut out the skirt pieces, and here's why. (We'll get to the how in just a few minutes.) Woven fabric is made of lengthwise and crosswise threads. In a perfect world, the crosswise threads are perpendicular to the lengthwise threads. The direction of these threads is called the *grain*. Your pattern pieces must follow the proper direction of the grain so your skirt hangs correctly. Most garment pieces follow the lengthwise (or straight) grain, because the lengthwise threads are designed to be stronger to withstand the tension of the weaving process. Some of the skirts in this book are cut along the *bias*; the bias flows along the diagonal between the lengthwise and crosswise threads. Garments cut on the bias have wonderful drape and cling to the body because this is the direction in which fabric has the most stretch.

The finished border on the length of the fabric is the *selvage*. This border differs in appearance from fabric to fabric. Most cutting layouts will have you fold the fabric lengthwise with the selvages aligned; smooth out the fabric so it's flat. If you can't get the wrinkles out and the fabric won't lie flat, you may need to straighten the crosswise edges and try again. Why? Sometimes the length

of the fabric wasn't perfectly cut along a crosswise thread.

If you're starting to get that creepy home ec feeling, chill: this is easier than it sounds, I promise. To find a crosswise thread, clip into the selvage and pull out a crosswise thread across the entire width of the fabric. Then, trim the edge even along this visible line, as you see so easily done below. Fold the fabric again, aligning the crosswise ends and the selvages; the ends and the selvages should be perpendicular to one another. Now that you're educated about fabric preparation, you're ready for the next step.

Straighten the fabric ends, as shown here.

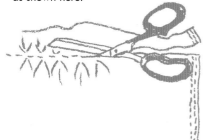

Prepare the pattern pieces

Grab your pattern and take out the pattern tissue and the instruction sheet. Look for your skirt letter (let's say Skirt B), and you'll find a listing of all the pieces you need for Skirt B. Cut the pieces you need from the large sheets of tissue; be sure to cut out the proper sizes. If you're using a multi-size pattern, which you probably are, you might want to highlight your cutting line. To remove the wrinkles from the pattern pieces after you've cut them from the large pieces of tissue, press each piece with a dry iron set on low heat.

Let's look at the pattern pieces themselves for a moment. Some pieces will be cut on the fold, which will be indicated by a pair of arrows pointing to the edge of the pattern. These are very easy to place correctly. Other pieces will be cut on the straight grain, indicated by a straight line with arrows on either end. These arrows must be parallel to the selvage so the fabric piece is cut on the straight grain. You insure this by measuring from each end of the arrow and adjusting until each end is the same distance from the selvage. Some pieces, such as facings, are often cut out from both fabric and interfacing, and this too will be indicated on the pattern piece. (A facing gets very lonely if you forget to cut its interfacing, so take note.)

Cut these notches.

Mark this dart and circle below.

Measure from this arrow.

Cut these notches, too!

And here's a typical skirt back. It has a couple of features that need to be marked, the dart and the circle. The arrow indicates it will be cut on the straight grain. All the notches should be cut, as you'll need to match them when you make the skirt.

Fold the fabric

Find the cutting layout for Skirt B according to your size and your fabric width. Place your fabric on a flat surface and align it properly as discussed on the previous pages, following the directions in your pattern's cutting layout. Sewing gurus disagree on whether to fold the right side of your fabric (the face) to the inside or outside; sometimes you need to be able to see the pattern on the fabric, so the face should be on the outside. However, it's probably most convenient to fold the right side to the inside for a couple of reasons. First, it's easy to mark with the wrong sides outside, and second, the right sides need to be facing when you sew anyway. Before you start to pin the pieces to the fabric, place them all on the fabric to make sure you understand the layout.

Pin in place

Keep fiddling around with the pieces until the measurements agree and your piece follows the straight grain. Pin the grainline arrows and the foldline arrows in place first and then pin the edges of each piece,

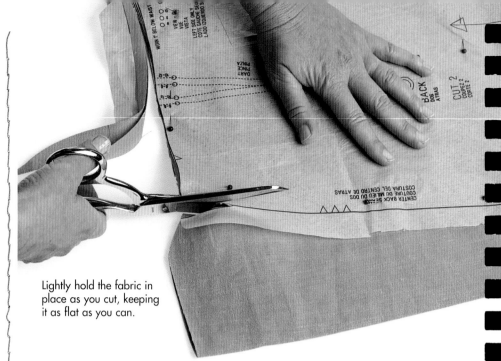

Lightly hold the fabric in place as you cut, keeping it as flat as you can.

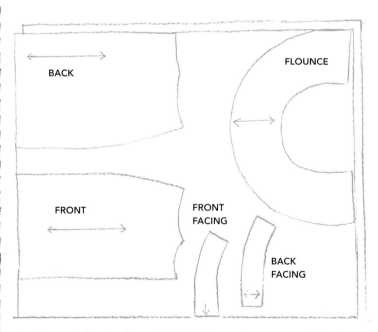

Here's a typical cutting layout. This is similar to the one we used for the Flirty Flounce skirt (page 60). The pieces that have arrows at the edge are cut on the fold, and those with straight arrows are cut on the lengthwise (straight) grain. Remember to cut the correct number of each piece.

with the pins on a diagonal facing into the corners. Finally, pin around the edge of each piece. The sewing gurus also give some differing advice about pinning, but most suggest placing all the pins perpendicular to the cut edge. To begin, how about pinning them the way that's most comfortable for you? Pin all the pieces in place before you cut the first one and refer to your layout to be sure you've placed each of the pieces for your skirt.

Cut out the skirt

Keep the fabric flat as you work, holding the pattern piece in place with your free hand as you cut. The notches you see are important markers for you when you're making your skirt; these help you properly match the various pieces when you're stitching them together. While you can cut them outward, I've found that it can be tricky to keep the fabric flat while you navigate the scissors around them, so I zip right through the notches and cut them inward after I've cut the piece out. This method saves a little time, too. Be mindful that there are single, double, and even triple notches, so cut them as such. You'll match single notches to single notches, double notches to double notches, and so on.

Use a ruler as a guide when you mark a straight line.

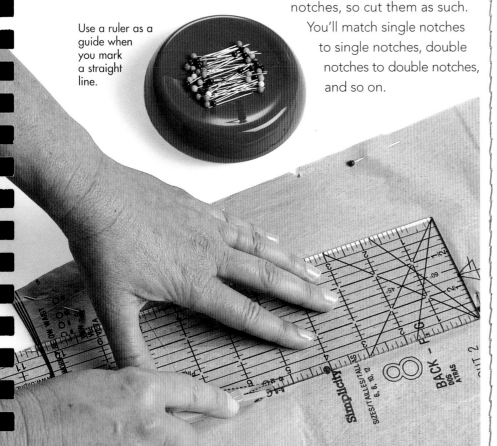

Mark the fabric

Your pattern pieces may have marks such as circles, darts, or pleats that need to be transferred to the wrong side of the fabric. The simplest way to do this is to use dressmaker's tracing paper and a tracing wheel. Usually, you can mark both pieces at the same time, unless the fabric is textured or heavyweight. Remove as few pins as possible to allow you to access the area you need to mark. Place the colored side of the paper to the wrong side of the fabric and trace over the markings with the wheel. If you're transferring straight lines, a ruler can be useful in accurately tracing the lines and keeping the pattern tissue in the proper position.

There are many tools to mark fabric. If you need to transfer only a dot, you can mark it with a fabric marking pen or chalk pencil. Be sure to test the markers you use on a scrap of fabric to be certain you can remove the marks if necessary. Because you may sometimes have to mark a placement line on the right side of the fabric, it's important to test your markers.

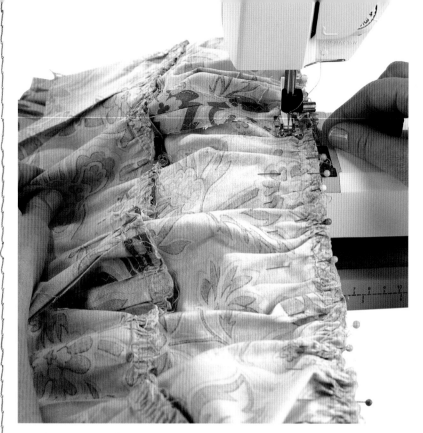

Stitching the tiers of the Gloriously Gathered skirt (page 76).

Start to sew

Okay, girlfriends, we're ready to sew. I hope you're as excited as I am! We've chosen a pattern, purchased the fabric and notions, and cut out and marked the skirt. Read through the next section and promise me you'll sit down at the sewing machine and practice stitching before you get started. Remember to familiarize yourself with your sewing machine and its controls (did I already tell you this?), and set up your workspace so all your tools and materials are handy.

In the following section, we'll talk about the basic techniques that we've used in our skirts. Don't try to remember everything at once, but read it through so you have a general understanding of the process. Later, in the Make a Skirt! section, you'll see how the techniques work in context when you make your skirt. We've presented them here with contrasting stitching so you can easily see what happens during each

step. Furthermore, we've used fabric that's similar (in some cases identical) to what we used for our skirts (linen, and a linen/rayon blend), so you can see real-world examples of how these fabrics behave when they're sewn. This isn't airbrushed sewing we're doing here.

And you may notice real-world sewing in the Make a Skirt! section, too—fabrics fray when they're handled and some techniques (like gathering) put more stress on the fabric, so you'll probably see a thread or two. You'll see them on your own skirts, too. Since you're learning, you shouldn't be overly stressed out about what the inside of your garment looks like, but do tidy up your skirt when you're done, trimming all the loose threads. This isn't work now—it's fun and you're just beginning. So plug in the machine, turn on the lights, and let's sew. If you need a refresher course when you're making your skirt, you can always flip back to these illustrated techniques.

Stitch a seam

To avoid boggling your mind unnecessarily, we've kept the sewing fairly simple in *Stylish Skirts*, using only basic techniques. There are three stitches: the *straight stitch*, the *basting stitch*, and the *zigzag*. The straight stitch is the foundation of your skirt; you can also do the straight stitch in reverse to anchor the beginning of your seams or to provide reinforcement at certain points, such as a zipper opening. (Consult our friend the manual for reverse stitching.) The basting stitch is simply a straight stitch set to a longer length. Use basting stitches to temporarily hold layers together or to gather fabric. Zigzag stitches are used to finish the raw edges of seams or for just plain fun.

Our 3 helpful stitches.

3. The straight stitch

2. The basting stitch

1. The zigzag

When you're practicing, use a contrasting thread so you can easily see what's happening. Also, use two pieces of fabric for the best results; sewing machines are designed to join two layers of fabric, so the top and bobbin stitches meet in the middle. Refer to You Know What for the proper way to thread your machine, wind the bobbin, and accurately set the stitch length. A setting of 10-12 stitches per inch is average for garment sewing.

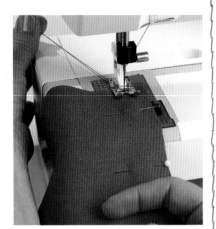

Gently hold the threads when you begin stitching.

To sew a seam, align the fabric edges and pin them together with the pins perpendicular to the fabric, heads near the edge. Line up the fabric to the ⅝-inch guideline on your sewing machine's needle plate; ⅝-inch seam allowances are standard in garment sewing. Place the fabric underneath the needle just a tiny bit (oh, ¼ inch) from the end of fabric. Lower the presser foot (do remember to do this because gnarly things happen if you forget). Hold the bobbin and top threads while you backstitch a couple of stitches to the end of the seam. Let go of the threads and stitch forward, pausing to remove the pins as you go. Don't, don't, *don't* be tempted to stitch over the pins—you can break a needle, or worse, ruin

Let the machine do the work while you guide the fabric. Remove the pins before you reach them.

your machine's timing by hitting a pin. Or even worse, have shards of metal flying around you and your skirt.

Guide the fabric lightly with your hands, keeping it straight against the guideline on your needle plate. Watch the guideline and not the needle—it can be hypnotizing. (You may think I'm kidding, but I'm not!) Let the machine do the work of pulling the fabric along (that's what those busy little feed dogs do). When you reach the end of the seam, backstitch for a few stitches to secure.

Congratulations—you stitched your first seam.
Relax and have a latte.

Balance the tension

After your latte (and maybe a snack), take a moment to admire your first seam. Look at both sides of the fabric; the stitches should look nearly identical on each side, being locked between the two pieces of fabric. If they don't look identical, you may need to adjust the thread tension on your machine. Each thread (top and bobbin) has its own tension. You may need to make adjustments to the tension according to the type of fabric you're using to make your skirt. Every time you sew with a new fabric, you should check the tension first.

The examples at the right show correct tension; top tension that's too tight; and top tension that's too loose. When the top tension is too tight, it yanks the poor bobbin thread up to the right side of the fabric; the opposite happens when the top tension is too loose. Following the instructions in (guess what?) your manual, make small adjustments at a time and do test seams until you're happy with the tension setting.

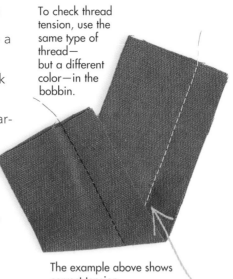

To check thread tension, use the same type of thread—but a different color—in the bobbin.

The example above shows correct tension.

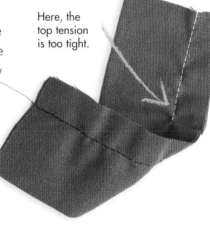

Here, the top tension is too tight.

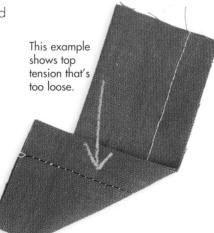

This example shows top tension that's too loose.

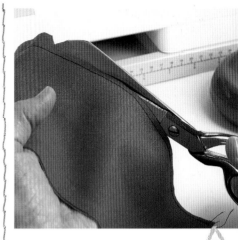

Trim seams and clip curves

At certain points along the way you'll need to trim a seam. Your pattern instructions will tell you when to do this. Generally, you trim a seam to reduce bulk in the finished garment (at the waistline of your skirt, for example). Simply use your shears to trim away the seam allowance to about ¼ inch.

Sometimes when you trim a seam you also need to clip the curves every inch or so. You'll see this often in our *Stylish Skirts* after the waistline has been stitched. Clipping allows a curved seam to spread and press flat. On inward curves—the kind we have in our skirts—simply use the tips of the scissors to clip just to the seam. Be careful not to clip through the stitching, of course. There's a clipped seam allowance on the next page.

Clipping to the
seamline

These techniques can be
used after the seam has been
stitched.

Finish the seams

To prevent raveling and make your skirt last longer, finish the
exposed seam allowances. You can do this before or after you
stitch the seam, depending on the method you choose. Let's talk
briefly about the various finishes.

ZIGZAG. If you want to finish the seams before you sew, sew a line
of zigzag stitching into the seam allowance, as close to the cut
edge as you can. This is a good choice for fabrics that tend to
ravel easily. After stitching the seam, press it open. If you're using
a lightweight fabric, you might find
that it's a little tricky to stitch
into the single thickness
without the fabric
puckering, so
use one
of the
methods
that follow
instead.

DOUBLE-STITCHED.
The double-stitched
seam is suitable
for lightweight
fabrics. After the
seam has been sewn, stitch
a parallel line of stitching in
the seam allowance, then
trim away close to the second line of stitching. Press
to one side.

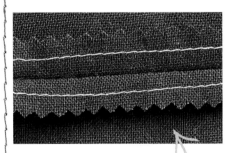

PINKED. This is a good
choice for tightly woven
fabrics. Stitch about ¼ inch
from the raw edge and then
trim with pinking shears.
Press open to finish.

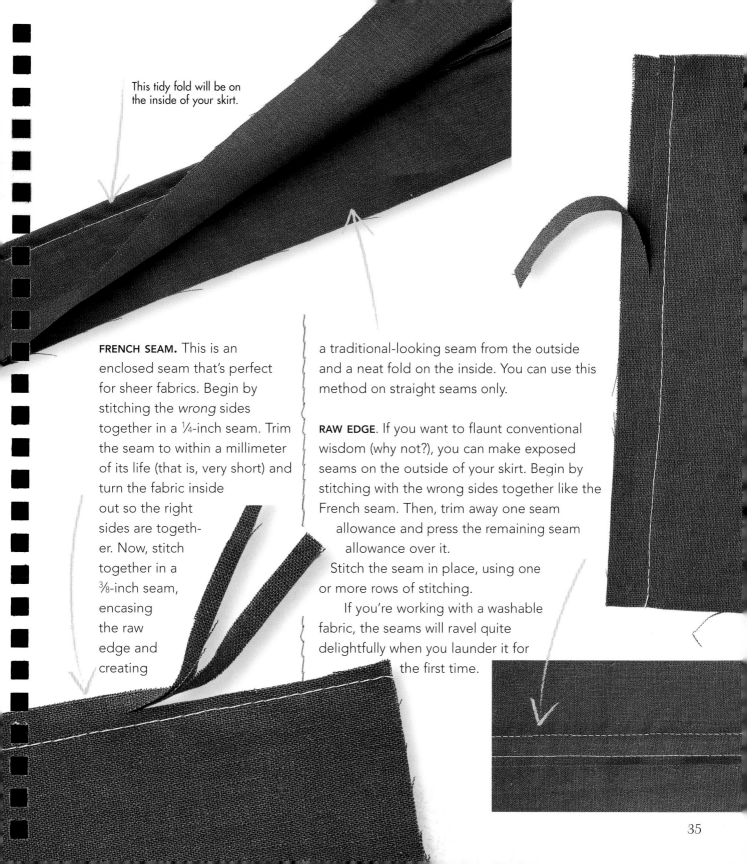

This tidy fold will be on the inside of your skirt.

FRENCH SEAM. This is an enclosed seam that's perfect for sheer fabrics. Begin by stitching the *wrong* sides together in a ¼-inch seam. Trim the seam to within a millimeter of its life (that is, very short) and turn the fabric inside out so the right sides are together. Now, stitch together in a ⅜-inch seam, encasing the raw edge and creating a traditional-looking seam from the outside and a neat fold on the inside. You can use this method on straight seams only.

RAW EDGE. If you want to flaunt conventional wisdom (why not?), you can make exposed seams on the outside of your skirt. Begin by stitching with the wrong sides together like the French seam. Then, trim away one seam allowance and press the remaining seam allowance over it.

Stitch the seam in place, using one or more rows of stitching.

If you're working with a washable fabric, the seams will ravel quite delightfully when you launder it for the first time.

Right sides together

Despite what I just said (don't you hate that?), you'll almost always sew the pieces of your skirt with the right sides together (facing each other). This is the most basic fact you need to remember about garment sewing if your seams are to be hidden away inside your skirt. If your fabric doesn't have easily recognizable right and wrong sides, be sure to mark each piece so you can quickly determine which is which, 'cause it's important.

Match notches

Remember when we cut the notches? Patterns include a series of notches to insure that you sew the right pieces (and the right *sides* of the pieces) to one another. If the notches don't seem to line up as the pattern instructions show, you may have one piece facing the wrong way, or you may be trying to pin the wrong edge of a piece. The notches should match exactly. Studying your pattern carefully will help you understand the proper orientation of the pieces.

Staystitch

This will generally be your first step in making a skirt. *Staystitching* is simply a line of stitching sewn ½ inch into the seam allowance to stabilize the piece. Staystitching is usually done on pieces that have curves, such as the waistline of a skirt. Staystitching is designed to be permanent (unlike most boyfriends).

Make a dart

Darts shape a skirt so it conforms to your body, so darts are your friends. Stitching a dart often follows the staystitching step when you're making a skirt. If your pattern calls for a dart, mark it carefully. You'll see that there's a peak in the center of the dart; fold the fabric at the peak and match any markings. Pin in place and stitch, beginning at the wide end of the dart. When you get to the narrow end of the dart, take a few stitches at the fold, but don't backstitch. Backstitching prevents the dart from lying flat. Instead, cut the threads long enough to tie into a knot to secure the end of the dart. Your pattern will tell you which direction to press the dart; it's usually toward the center.

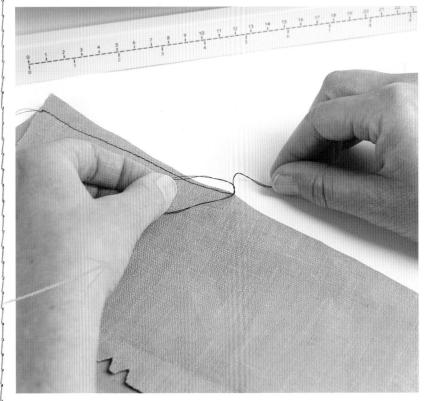

Install a zipper

Skirts with elasticized waists are wonderful, because they're comfy and easy to make. But eventually—perhaps even this afternoon—you'll want to make a fitted skirt. Of course you've got to get into (and out of) said fitted skirt, so you need to learn to install a zipper. A zipper is a wonderful device, so let's figure it out.

There are several ways to put in a zipper, but the standard for skirts is the lapped zipper. We may as well learn this method because it's not the least bit hard. Our version calls for a zipper that's a couple of inches longer than the pattern asks for. This technique eliminates some fumbling around with the zipper pull during installation as well as the need for a hook and eye closure. (If you've never fumbled around with a zipper pull, you're lucky; if you have, you know exactly what I'm talking about.) Be sure to buy a zipper with nylon coils (*not* metal) because you have to trim off the excess and stitch right over it, too.

You install a zipper in a seam that is partially sewn. Most patterns will have you stitch to a notch or a marked circle. Let's pretend that we've done that, too.

For a fitted skirt, you've got to have a zipper! Your hips demand it.

1 After stitching the seam to the appropriate spot, back-stitch for a few stitches to anchor it. On the right opening edge, press under the seam allowance to ½ inch. Press under the left opening edge to the seamline, ⅝ inch.

2 Place the closed zipper under the right edge, placing the zipper stop at the notch or the marked spot. Have the zipper teeth close to the pressed edge of the fabric. Pin the zipper in place at the end of the zipper tape. Put the zipper foot on your sewing machine and baste this side of the zipper in place (photo 1); it doesn't have to be close to the zipper teeth just yet. Change the stitch length to a normal setting and adjust your zipper foot so you can stitch close to the fabric edge and the zipper teeth (photo 2).

3 Lap the left opening edge over the right (photo 3) and baste in place, as in step 2.

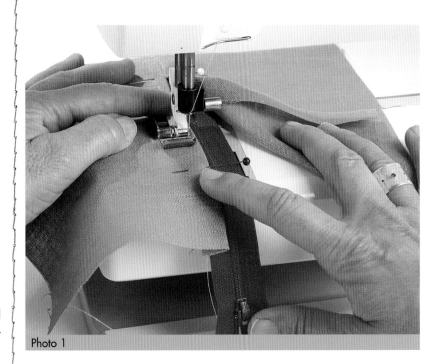
Photo 1

Photo 2

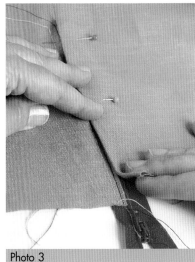
Photo 3

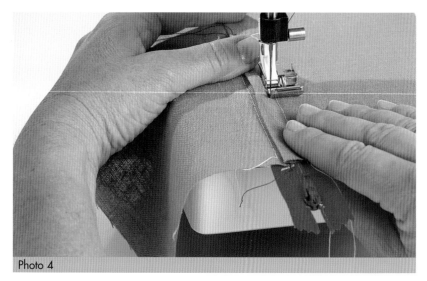
Photo 4

4 Reduce the stitch length and adjust your zipper foot to stitch the left side of the zipper in place; you won't need to stitch quite as close to the pressed edge on this side. Begin at the seam and stitch across the lapped end. *Pivot* the fabric by stopping with the needle in the fabric, lifting the presser foot, and turning to stitch up the right side (photo 4). Remember to put the presser foot back down after you pivot!

Photo 5

5 Remove the basting stitches (photo 5). Your zipper's just about finished (photo 6).

6 Lower the zipper pull and trim off the excess zipper (photo 7). The raw end of the zipper tape will be encased in the facing or waistband of your skirt.

Almost done!
Photo 6

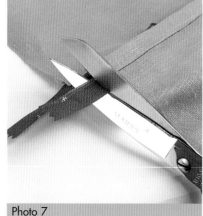
Photo 7

This facing has been understitiched—here's the line of stitiching.

Understitch the facings

Understitching is used on facings to make them behave and stay out of sight on the inside of a garment. After the seam has been trimmed and clipped, press the seam allowance toward the facing. From the right side, stitch close to the seamline through all layers of the facing. After understitching, turn the facing to the inside.

Here the facing has been pressed to the inside of the skirt.

Ease to fit

Sometimes, to insure the proper fit or drape, you'll sew one piece to another that's ever-so-slightly longer. This is called *easestitching*, created by gently gathering a portion of the longer piece.

Easestitching is done with a row of basting stitches that are pulled to fit, with the fullness distributed in the seam allowance and not visible in the skirt.

You can also ease the fullness of a hem, as you'll see on page 96.

Make a narrow hem

Most of the skirts in this book are finished with narrow hems. It's just like it sounds: a skinny little hem that's stitched in place on the machine. Typically they're made like this: Stitch ⅜ inch from the lower edge of the skirt and press up along this line of stitching. Tuck under the raw edge to meet the stitching, forming a nice fold. Press and stitch in place along the fold.

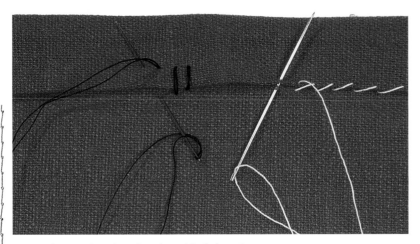

Hemstitches in white thread; tacks in black thread.

Stitch by hand

You only need a few basic hand stitches to complete these skirts. A basic *hemstitch* can multitask to secure facings at the zipper as well as to hem your skirt. A *tack* will hold facings to seam allowances.

Begin with a knot in your thread; make a simple loop in the end and pull the needle through. Sometimes a second knot is necessary to keep the thread from pulling through the fabric. A hemstitch is begun with the needle inserted into the fold of the fabric. Work from right to left as you pick up just a thread or two in the skirt and then insert the needle into the edge of the fold above the first stitch. Repeat, making stitches every ¼ inch or so.

Finish a line of hand stitching in one of two ways. Make a series of *backstitches* (a small stitch made from left to right and repeated several times in place). You can also make a quick knot. Make a wee stitch on top of your last stitch on the wrong side of your fabric, forming a small loop. Pull the needle through the loop until a second loop forms. Pull the needle through the second loop tightly to form a knot.

A *tack* is simply a straight stitch used to join layers of fabric; you can repeat them in place or make a series of straight stitches. You'll use them in your skirts to anchor facings to seam allowances. Make sure your tacks don't go through the skirt itself, just the facings and seam allowances.

Check the fit

Try on the skirt after each major step, such as when the side seams are sewn and the waistband added. Don't wait until the skirt has been completed, because it will take a lot of sweat and even more tears to unmake it if you need to tweak the fit. Remember that it's better to err on the side of being too big than too small when you're deciding on a size. If you need to make the skirt smaller, do so in teeny increments, such as ⅛ inch. Exhibit A: If you're taking in the side seams, this seemingly tiny measurement translates into ¼ inch on each side of the skirt and ½ inch for the entire skirt.

If you're stressed about fit, use the traditional couture approach of making a *muslin*. A muslin is a sample garment that's made of inexpensive material (i.e., cotton muslin) for the purpose of testing fit. The sample garment need only have the major pieces stitched together, with no seam finishes or completed details. A perk with making a muslin is that you can practice sewing before you begin your actual skirt. Then you're tweaking the muslin, and not your precious fabric. With a muslin, you'll be confident your skirt will fit after you've invested time and money in it.

Fix a mistake

The best way to fix a mistake is to avoid it in the first place (excuse me if I'm beginning to sound like your mother). But of course, we all make them, even the most experienced seamstresses. There's not much that can't be repaired by simply ripping out all the stitches and trying again. When you're using a seam ripper to remove stitches, be careful not to tear the fabric by ripping too enthusiastically. I know how much fun it can be (!).

If you're having a weak moment and feel unsure about something you've just stitched, chill a second and make sure it's correct before you trim the seam allowances or clip the curves.

Photo 1

Photo 2

Photo 3

Embellish Your Skirt

Most of the skirts you love are likely to have some sort of embellishment—lovely ribbon, funky rickrack, or whatever suits your fancy. Several of our stylish skirts are so decorated, and you can choose to include these embellishments as you wish. (But why wouldn't you? It's easy.) Even if your pattern doesn't call for trim or a decorative technique, you can still include them if you want. Here's the scoop on adding accoutrements to the skirts in this book.

If your skirt is constructed in panels, you can decorate each seam with trim. Center the trim atop the seam, and pin it in place if you'd like. Adding the trim gives you another opportunity to be creative—will you use a complementary thread, or choose a contrasting one for pizzazz?

You can sew it in place with a simple straight stitch along both edges of the trim (photo 1), add a decorative stitch down the center (photo 2), or even layer trims to add a personal touch. When you're actually stitching on the trim, sew at a medium speed so you can easily guide the trim.

Pinning the trim in place makes a lot of sense if you don't have a seam to follow, or if you have several pieces of trim to coordinate, or if you're just picky. To decorate one of our skirts, rickrack was added around the yoke after being pinned in place first (photo 3). If you pin the trim to your skirt, remove the pins as you come to them. (Remember, no stitching over the pins!)

You can add trim before you finish the skirt, or after. If you add trim before the skirt is complete, the raw ends of the trim are usually hidden inside a facing or turned under to the hem, for example. If you add trim after the skirt is finished, you'll need to hide the raw ends of the trim, if you care about that kind of thing.

Photo 4

When you cut the trim, remember to add an extra ½ inch or so for tidying the ends, folding under one end to cover the other (photo 4). If you want a deconstructed look, simply add the trim without turning under the ends. What the heck.

Another easy way you can enliven your skirt is to use contrasting fabrics. We used this trick to add fabric "ribbons" and a bright band for visual interest (photo 5).

The fabrics we used had the same print, but were in a different colorway. When you're shopping for multiple fabrics to use in a project, be sure to take a swatch along with you. If your pattern calls for ribbon, keep in mind that you can use fabric to make your own custom trim.

Exposed seams add depth and dimension to a garment (photo 6). Remember, we gave you one method for making them on page 35, which depended on washing the skirt to make the edges bloom. But you can also make cool frayed edges in other easy ways, too. Here's a simple method that works without the washing step: after you stitch the seam (with the wrong sides together, of course, so it shows on the outside), use a toothbrush to fluff the raw edges.

For your reading pleasure, we've included some additional techniques you can use to embellish your skirts on page 100. It's free with the purchase of *Stylish Skirts*!

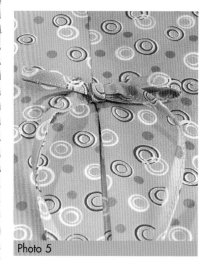

Photo 5

Photo 6

45

Use This Book

Alright, ladies, we've discussed just about everything you really need to know about making a skirt. We've looked at how-to photographs and illustrations. I'm just about ready to turn it over to you. Here's how the projects in this book will help you make your own skirt when you're ...

CHOOSING YOUR PATTERN. Because I think much of the fun is in finding the pattern, I won't insist that you use the same design we did in the projects that follow. Why not? Because patterns are tied to fashion trends just like ready-to-wear garments in stores, so the companies update their offerings and discontinue patterns as the market dictates—a perfectly reasonable business practice. To allow for changing trends, the instructions give you enough information to find a pattern that has similar features to the one we used (and you smart chicks will probably find patterns that suit you even better than the ones we used). We've included illustrations of the patterns we used on page 110.

FOLLOWING THE INSTRUCTIONS. Purchase the fabric and notions as your pattern instructs. We'll give you the directions that we used to make our skirts, including some tips and witty explanations for some of the techniques. (Commercial patterns assume that you have a basic knowledge of sewing, so sometimes a little extra information is oh-so-helpful.) Our illustrated how-to instructions will complement the directions in your pattern envelope. If your pattern has similar features to ours, the directions should be somewhat alike, too. The basic instructions in *Stylish Skirts* (such as installing a zipper or understitching a waistband) should apply to just about any pattern that has similar construction.

ANALYZING OUR PROJECTS. Generally speaking, the skirts are presented in categories according to ease of construction, beginning with a basic pull-on skirt. The icons will rate the ease of the pattern, and the key on page 49 explains which skills are included in each category. As the skirts progress, techniques are added so you'll have gained a repertoire of sewing skills by the end of the book. Once you understand a technique—making a narrow hem, for example—you can apply it to any project. See pages 50 and 51 for a quick preview of each skirt.

PREPARING TO SEW. Now that you've got everything you need to begin sewing, arrange your tools and materials within easy reach. And there's nothing worse than squinting while you're sewing, so treat yourself to adequate lighting in your workspace.

Speaking of tools and materials, you'll see a list for each of our skirt projects. However, we're not going to list *every* supply you need for each skirt, but rather refer you to this list of basic skirt-making tools and materials. Have the following on hand for any little number in our Make a Skirt! section:

sewing machine

machine needles

measuring tools

marking tools

scissors

seam ripper

pins

needles for hand sewing

thread

Of course, you'll also need any additional notions suggested by your pattern.

Only a few more pages of handy information and we'll be ready to rid the world of skirt envy!

Anatomy of a *Skirt*

Here's a quick visual recap of the skirt-making process. Could it be any easier?

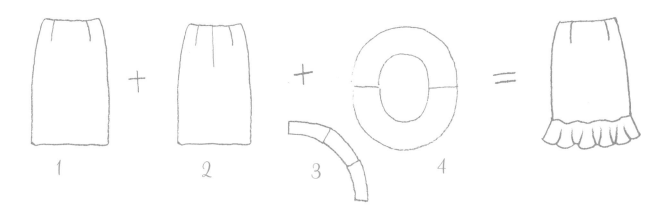

1   +   2   +   3   4

1 Staystitch the edges and make the darts in the front.

2 Staystitch the back sections, stitch them together partway, and add the zipper.

3 Stitch the facing sections together and sew it to the waistline.

4 Stitch the flounce sections together, make a narrow hem in the flounce, and stitch to the skirt.

Presto! Your very own handmade skirt. Wear proudly.

Each of our projects is rated according to ease of construction. (Please note that I didn't say *difficulty* of construction.) Here's how we've organized them.

Icon Key

ABSOLUTE BEGINNER

Suitable for the first-time sewer.

BASIC SKILLS YOU'LL USE:

Matching notches (page 36)

Narrow hem (page 41)

Right sides together (page 36)

EASY BEGINNER

Suitable for the new sewer who understands the basics and is ready to install a zipper.

NEW SKILLS YOU'LL USE:

Install a zipper (page 38)

Seam finishes (page 34)

Hand stitches (page 42)

Staystitching (page 37)

Trim seams and clip curves (page 33)

Understitching (page 41)

EXPERIENCED BEGINNER

Suitable for the sewer who's mastered the zipper and is ready to sew at warp speed.

NEW SKILLS YOU'LL USE:

Easing to fit (page 41)

French seams (page 35)

Tip

A tip offers you a nifty idea.

Why?

Wondering why you're doing something? Here's the answer.

Runway Preview

Here's the scoop on the skirts you'll see in our collection that begins on page 52. Aren't you excited?

1 POLKA DOT PERFECTION

See how great a simple pattern can look when you choose a fantastic fabric. This basic pull-on skirt with an elasticized waist is anything *but* boring.

2 SIMPLY STYLISH

Next up is an elasticized skirt with cool extras; you'll add some hip details such as a drawstring waist and an unfinished hem.

3 FLIRTY FLOUNCE

Add a zipper to make a fitted straight skirt; add a flounce to make heads turn. The zipper allows you to make a fitted skirt; the flounce assures attraction.

4 EASILY EMBELLISHED

After achieving zipper enlightenment, stitch a few panels and add some trim for decoration. The panels in this skirt offer lots of sewing practice and the simple ribbon trim adds style.

5 INTENTIONALLY ASYMMETRICAL

Go for the deconstructed look with mod exposed seams and a raveled hem. The funky (but fun) sections in this skirt give you experience with matching notches and markings.

6 **ELEGANTLY EDGY**

Play with a great design, combining vintage rickrack and modern details with a classic fabric. This is the first of several skirts that are constructed with a yoke.

7 **GLORIOUSLY GATHERED**

Gather sections of fabric to make the multiple tiers in this carefree skirt. Adorn it with lots of complementary trim, please.

8 **LUSCIOUSLY LAYERED**

Double the pleasure with a skirt constructed of layers of luxurious fabric. A simple ribbon technique finishes the waist.

9 **SOPHISTICATED SIMPLICITY**

Pleats are a classic tailoring detail, but contrasting fabric trim makes this skirt lively and so *not* yesterday.

10 **ARTFULLY ARRANGED**

This lined skirt lets you use see-through eyelet and the tulle trim adds pizzazz.

Now let's get busy & make a skirt!

You're lucky
I waited.

Polka Dot *Perfection*

*Whip up a new look with a simple pattern,
a fabulous fabric, and a little attitude.*

WHAT YOU NEED

Pattern for a bias-cut,
pull-on skirt

Fabric and notions per the
pattern envelope (we used
cotton fabric, contrasting
thread, and ½-inch elastic)

Basic skirt-making tools and
materials (page 47)

Bodkin

 ABSOLUTE BEGINNER

Cheat sheet for absolute
beginner on page 49

Pattern schematics on page 110

HOW YOU MAKE IT

1 Cut out and mark the
skirt according to your
pattern's instructions.
Remember to finish the
seam allowances of your
skirt, using the method of
your choice.

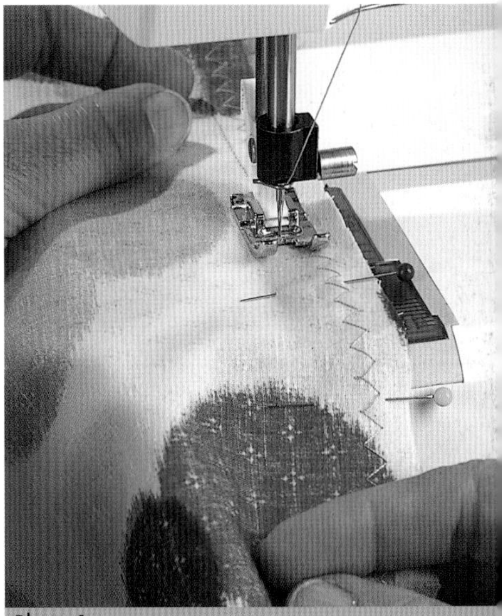

2 Stitch the skirt front and
back sections together
at the side seams, right sides
together, matching the
notches (photo 1).

3 In the next step, you're
going to make a casing
for the elasticized waist.
First, to save yourself the frustration of getting the elastic stuck
in the casing when you insert it in the casing, begin
by basting the upper 3 or 4 inches of the side seam allowances
to the skirt (a peek of this step appears in photo 2 on the
next page).

Photo 1

Photo 2

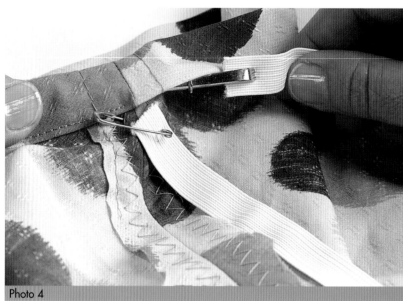

Photo 4

Photo 3

Photo 5

4 Make the casing by pressing 1 inch of the upper edge of the skirt to the inside. Press under ¼ inch on the raw edge. Stitch close to the lower edge of the casing, leaving an opening to insert the elastic (photo 2). Note the line of basting stitches from step 3, visible at the seam.

5 Cut a piece of elastic to fit your waist, plus 1 inch. Pin the free end of the elastic to the skirt so it doesn't disappear inside the casing and insert the other end of the elastic through the casing using a bodkin (photos 3 and 4). Overlap the ends and pin them together so you can try on the skirt. Adjust the elastic to fit if necessary.

6 Stitch the ends of elastic together securely (photo 5) and stitch the opening closed. Distribute the fullness evenly through the waist. Remove the basting stitches at the seam allowances. (If you want, you can secure the elastic in place by stitching through the casing at each side seam.)

7 Let the skirt hang overnight. Try it on and mark the desired length. If necessary, trim the depth of the hem evenly, allowing ⅜ inch for a narrow hem. Stitch ⅜ inch from the lower edge of the skirt. Press up the hem along this line of stitching, then tuck under the raw edge to meet the line of stitching. Press. Stitch the hem in place (photo 6).

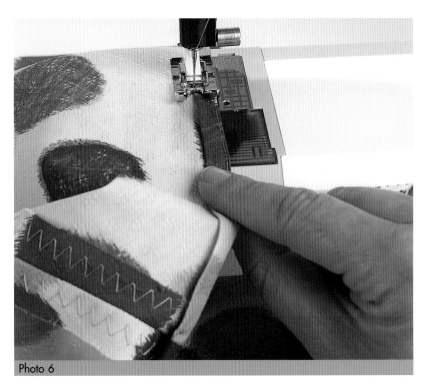

Photo 6

Why?

When you cut woven fabric on the bias, it drapes beautifully because this is the direction in which the fabric has the most stretch. A skirt cut on the bias needs to hang to relax to its maximum length before you hem it.

Simply *Stylish*

For a sunny afternoon of errands, you need a breezy linen skirt with a casual unfinished hem and an easy drawstring waist.

WHAT YOU NEED

Pattern for a bias-cut, pull-on skirt with a drawstring waist

Fabric and notions per the pattern envelope (we used linen/rayon blend fabric, matching thread, and ⅜-inch elastic)

Basic skirt-making tools and materials (page 47)

Craft knife

Bodkin

ABSOLUTE BEGINNER

Cheat sheet for absolute beginner on page 49

Pattern schematics on page 110

HOW YOU MAKE IT

1 Cut out and mark the skirt according to your pattern's instructions. Remember to finish the seam allowances of your skirt, using the method of your choice.

2 The drawstring in this skirt exits the casing through a buttonhole. (Follow the instructions in your sewing machine's manual to make the buttonholes. If you've never made a buttonhole before, practice on some scraps of fabric before you begin.)

Cut one 1½ x 1-inch remnant of fabric to reinforce the underside of the buttonholes in the front of the skirt. Center the remnant over the buttonhole markings on the wrong side of the front and baste in place. Make the buttonholes at the markings and carefully slice open with a craft knife (photos 1 and 2).

Photo 1

Photo 2

The skirt's almost as cool as me.

3 Stitch the front and back sections together at the side seams, right sides together, matching the notches.

4 As with the previous skirt, you'll make a casing for the elasticized waist. To keep the elastic from frustrating you by getting stuck in the seam allowances when you insert it in the casing, begin by basting the upper 3 or 4 inches of the seam allowances to the skirt. Make the casing by pressing ¾ inch of the upper edge of the skirt to the inside. Press under ¼ inch on the raw edge. Stitch close to the lower edge of casing.

5 With the right sides together, fold each drawstring in half lengthwise. Turn the raw edges into the middle and press (photo 3). Stitch along the edge. Finish one end of each drawstring by folding under the raw edges and stitching.

6 Cut one piece of elastic approximately 19 inches long. Lap the ends of the elastic over the unfinished ends of each drawstring. Stitch securely (photo 4).

Photo 3

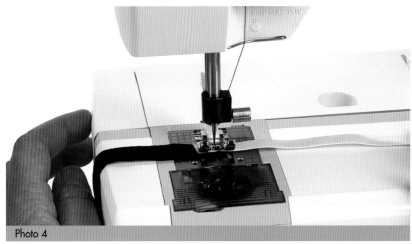
Photo 4

Photo 5

7 Insert the drawstring into the casing through the buttonhole openings, using the bodkin (photo 5).

8 Stitch the lower band sections together at the side seams, right sides together, matching the notches.

9 Mark the ⅝-inch seamlines on the wrong side of the skirt and the right side of the band. Lap the lower edge of the skirt over the band, matching the centers and the seamlines (photo 6). Stitch in place along the seamline (photo 7), marking the seamline as shown, if necessary.

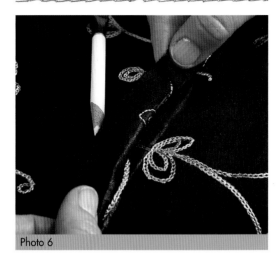
Photo 6

Tip

This pattern features a band that has an unfinished hem and a lapped seam with a raw edge. A band like this can easily be created from a pattern for a plain long skirt, too. Simply cut the pattern approximately 8 inches above the hem and use this separate piece to cut a band. Remember to add a ⅝-inch seam allowance to both the skirt and the band. Then overlap it and stitch as in step 9 above.

Photo 7

Mind if I taste
your drink?

Flirty Flounce

No wardrobe is complete unless it contains a skirt with a playful flounce; make yours in just a few hours.

WHAT YOU NEED

Pattern for a straight skirt with a zipper and a flounce

Fabric and notions per the pattern envelope (we used cotton fabric and matching thread)—*remember to buy a longer zipper*

Basic skirt-making tools and materials (page 47)

EASY BEGINNER

Cheat sheet for easy beginner on page 49

Pattern schematics on page 110

HOW YOU MAKE IT

1 Cut out and mark the skirt according to your pattern's instructions. Remember to finish the seam allowances of your skirt, using the method of your choice.

2 Staystitch the upper edge of the front ½ inch from the cut edge; be sure to stitch in the direction your pattern indicates. Make the darts in the front (photo 1); press them toward the center of the skirt.

3 Staystitch the upper edges of the back pieces ½ inch from the cut edge; be sure to stitch in the proper direction.

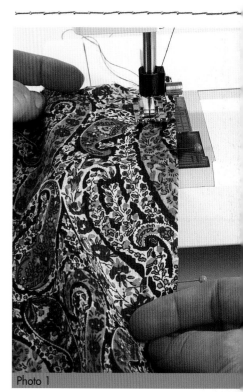

Photo 1

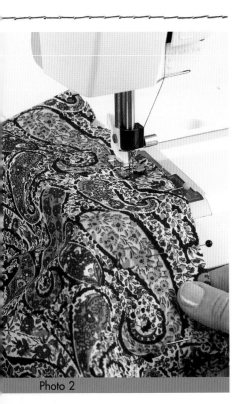

Photo 2

4 Make the darts in the back and press them toward the center of the skirt. Stitch the center back seam from the notch to the lower edge, right sides together, matching the notches (photo 2). Backstitch at the notch to reinforce the seam.

5 To install the zipper in the back, turn in ½ inch on the right opening edge; press. Turn in the left opening edge along the seamline and press. Place the closed zipper under the right opening edge, placing the zipper stop at the notch and the zipper teeth close to the pressed edge. Pin the end of the zipper tape to the skirt. Using a zipper foot, baste the zipper to the skirt and then stitch close to the edge (photo 3). Lap the left opening edge over the right opening edge, matching seamlines. Baste and then stitch in place, pivoting below the notch. Trim the excess length from the zipper.

6 Stitch the front to the back at the side seams, right sides together, matching the notches.

7 Now you'll add a facing to the waistline. Apply fusible interfacing to the facing sections following the manufacturer's directions. Stitch the side seams of the facing sections, right sides together. Finish the long unnotched edge by stitching ¼ inch from the edge; turn under along the stitching, press, and stitch.

8 With the right sides together, pin the facing to the skirt, matching the centers, the notches, and the side seams (photo 4). (The facing extends ½ inch beyond the right opening

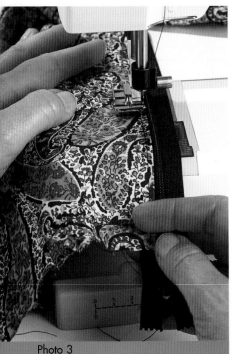

Photo 3

Photo 4

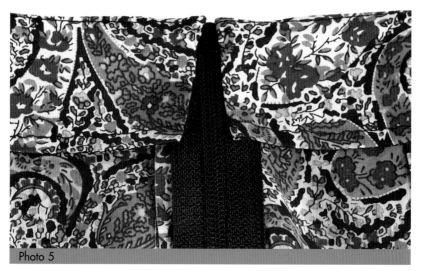
Photo 5

together. Stitch along the seam-line on the notched edge of the flounce so you can clip to this line of stitching in step 13.

12 Make a narrow hem at the lower edge of flounce: Stitch ⅜ inch from the lower edge. Press up the hem along this line of stitching, then tuck under the raw edge to meet the line of stitching. Press. Stitch the hem in place.

13 Clip the notched edge of the flounce to the line of stitching, being careful not to clip through the stitching. With the right sides together, pin the flounce to the lower edge of the skirt, matching first the side seams, then the centers, and lastly the notches (photo 6). Stitch. Press the seam toward the skirt, pressing the flounce out.

Photo 6

edge and ⅝ inch beyond the left opening edge.) Baste in place. Stitch along the seam-line. Trim the seam and clip the curves.

9 To understitch the facing, press it away from the skirt, pressing the seam toward the facing. With the facing side up, stitch close to the seam

through the facing and the seam allowances.

10 Turn the facing to the inside, turning under and hemstitching the edges to the zipper tape; press (photo 5). To keep the facing in place, tack it to the seam allowances.

11 Stitch the front and back flounce sections together at the side seams, right sides

Why

Clipping to the seamline enables you to spread the circular flounce to fit the straight skirt.

Easily *Embellished*

After learning the basics, experiment with trim and vintage fabric for a sizzling skirt.

Photo 1

Photo 2

HOW YOU MAKE IT

1 Cut out and mark the skirt according to your pattern's instructions. Because the trim will be stitched to the seam allowances, it's not necessary to finish them.

2 When you're stitching the panels together, be sure that you're correctly matching the notches. Begin by stitching the center seam of the front sections, right sides together (photo 1). Stitch the side front sections to the front section, right sides together.

3 Stitch each back section to a side back section. Stitch front to back at the side seams (photo 2). You'll stitch the center back seam later, after the trim is applied at the other seams.

WHAT YOU NEED

Pattern for an A-line skirt with a zipper and panels

Fabric and notions per the pattern envelope (we used vintage synthetic crepe, matching and contrasting thread, ribbon of varying widths, and ¼-inch twill tape)—*remember to buy a longer zipper*

Basic skirt-making tools and materials (page 47)

EASY BEGINNER

Cheat sheet for easy beginner on page 49

Pattern schematics on page 110

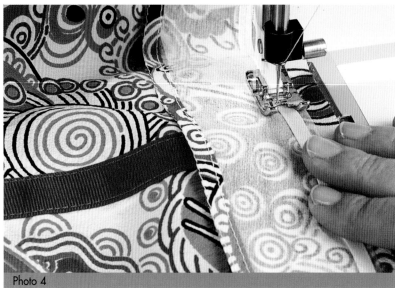

Photo 4

Photo 3

4 Measure and cut seven pieces of ribbon that are the length of the skirt. On the right side of the skirt, center a strip of ribbon along the center front seam and stitch in place, sewing close to both edges of the ribbon (photo 3). Repeat for the side front seams, the side seams, and the side back seams.

5 Stitch the center back seam from the lower edge to the notch, right sides together. Backstitch at the notch to reinforce the seam.

6 To install the zipper in the back, turn in ½ inch on the right opening edge; press. Turn in the left opening edge along the seamline and press. Place the closed zipper under the right opening edge, placing the zipper stop at the notch and the zipper teeth close to the pressed edge. Pin the end of the zipper tape to the skirt. Using a zipper foot, baste the zipper to the skirt and then stitch close to the edge. Lap the left opening edge over the right opening edge, matching seamlines. Baste and then

stitch in place, pivoting below the notch. Trim the excess length from the zipper.

7 Now you'll add a facing to the waistline. Apply fusible interfacing to the facing sections following the manufacturer's directions. Stitch the side seams of the facing sections, right sides together. Finish the long unnotched edge by stitching ¼ inch from the edge; turn under along the stitching, press, and stitch.

8 With the right sides together, pin the facing to the skirt, matching the centers and the side seams. (The facing extends ½ inch beyond the right opening edge and ⅝ inch beyond the left opening edge.)

Baste in place. To prevent stretching, baste a length of twill tape along the seamline (photo 4). Stitch along the seamline. Trim the seam and clip the curves. (Don't clip the tape.)

9 To understitch the facing, press it away from the garment, pressing the seam toward the facing. With the facing side up, stitch close to the seam through the facing and the seam allowances.

10 Turn the facing to the inside, turning under and hemstitching the edges to the zipper tape; press. To keep the facing in place, tack it to the seam allowances.

11 Make a narrow hem: Stitch ⅜ inch from the lower edge of the skirt. Press up the hem along this line of stitching, then tuck under the raw edge of the skirt (including the ribbon) to meet the line of stitching. Press. Stitch the hem in place (photo 5). You may need to adjust your presser foot pressure to stitch over the ribbon; consult your friendly sewing machine manual to make this adjustment.

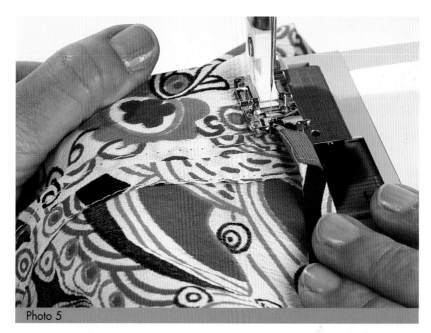

Photo 5

Photo 6

Tip

Let your muse guide you when choosing embellishments for your skirt. We used three different types of grosgrain ribbon for trim, using a contrasting zigzag stitch to apply the narrowest ribbon (photo 6).

I made dinner for eight ... and I'm still smiling.

Intentionally *Asymmetrical*

*The deconstructed seams on this richly colored
skirt add a hip detail to an easily constructed garment.*

Pattern for a mid-length skirt
with a zipper and sections

Fabric and notions per the
pattern envelope (we used a
washable linen/rayon blend,
matching and contrasting
thread, and ¼-inch twill
tape)—*remember to buy a
longer zipper*

Basic skirt-making tools and
materials (page 47)

EASY BEGINNER

Cheat sheet for easy
beginner on page 49

Pattern schematics on
page 110

HOW YOU MAKE IT

1 Cut out and mark the skirt
according to your pattern's
instructions—but you must cut
the notches *outward* on this
skirt. Finish the seam
allowances of the side seams
only, using the method of your
choice.

2 For the raw-edged seams
on the skirt front and
back, use this method: Stitch
each seam with the *wrong*
sides together. Trim away one
seam allowance (the lower
one, in this case) and press the
remaining seam allowance

Photo 1

over it. Stitch the seam in place, using one row of contrasting
stitching and one row of matching stitching (photo 1). There's a
secret to the raveled edges: after you wash the skirt, the
exposed seams fray joyfully. (If you need a refresher course, see
the illustrated instructions on page 35.)

3 Staystitch the upper edges of the front and the back ½ inch
from the cut edge; be sure to stitch in the direction your
pattern indicates.

4 With the wrong sides together, pin the middle front to the upper front, being sure to correctly match the notches (photo 2). Stitch, using the method described in step 2. With the wrong sides together, stitch the lower front to the middle front, again using the method described in step 2. (Not to be a nag, but be sure to match the notches carefully when you're sewing these all pieces together.)

5 Stitch the seams of the skirt back as you did the front, wrong sides together.

6 Now, *right* sides together, pin the front to the back at the side seams, stitching the left side seam from the lower edge to the notch, matching the seams (photo 3). Backstitch at the notch to reinforce the seam.

7 To install the zipper on the left side, turn in ½ inch on the back opening edge; press. Turn in the front opening edge along the seamline and press. Place the closed zipper under the back opening edge,

Photo 2

Photo 3

placing the zipper stop at the notch and the zipper teeth close to the pressed edge. Pin the end of the zipper tape to the skirt. Using a zipper foot, baste the zipper to the skirt and then stitch close to the edge. Lap the front opening edge over the back opening edge, matching seamlines. Baste and then stitch in place, pivoting below the notch. Trim the excess length from the zipper.

8 Now you'll add a facing to the waistline. Apply fusible interfacing to the facing sections following the manufacturer's directions. Stitch the right side seam of the facing sections, right sides together. Finish the long unnotched edge by stitching ¼ inch from the edge; turn under along the stitching, press, and stitch.

9 With right sides together, pin the facing to the skirt, matching the centers and the right side seams. (The facing extends ½ inch beyond the back opening edge and ⅝ inch beyond the front opening edge.) Baste in place. To prevent stretching, baste a length of twill tape along the seamline. Stitch along the seamline. Trim the seam and clip the curves. (Don't clip the tape.)

10 To understitch the facing, press it away from the skirt, pressing the seam toward the facing. With the facing side up, stitch close to the seam through the facing and the seam allowances.

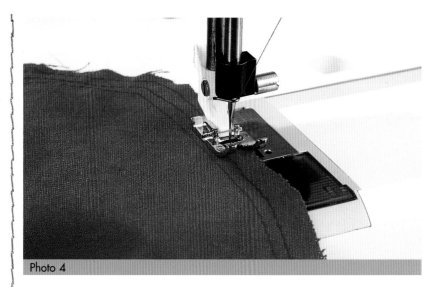
Photo 4

11 Turn the facing to the inside, turning under and hemstitching the edges to the zipper tape; press. To keep the facing in place, tack it to the seam allowances.

12 To finish the skirt, make three lines of parallel stitching at the bottom edge to mimic the seams, using a contrasting color in the middle. Leave the hem otherwise unfinished (photo 4).

Photo 5

Tip

If you want funky seams that ravel like these (photo 5), you must use a washable fabric. But you can still use this method for exposed seams on fabrics that must be dry-cleaned—see page 45 to learn how to add the fizz of the frayed material.

Elegantly Edgy

Designer details and a little bit of lighthearted rickrack create a personal style statement.

HOW YOU MAKE IT

1 Cut out and mark the skirt according to your pattern's instructions; we marked two placement lines on the yoke for the rickrack. We also chose to match the plaid on the yoke by aligning the notches (look for the cool blue pins in photo 1). When you match the notches along a stripe, the stripes will look continuous when you stitch the seam. If you use a fabric such as this novelty tweed, it's especially important to finish the seams *before sewing* to avoid excess raveling.

2 Staystitch the upper edge of the yoke front ½ inch from the cut edge; be sure to stitch in the direction your pattern indicates. Make the darts in the front and press them toward the center of the skirt.

3 Staystitch the upper edge of the yoke back ½ inch from the cut edge; be sure to stitch in the direction your pattern indicates. Make the darts in the back and press them toward the center of the skirt.

WHAT YOU NEED

Pattern for an A-line skirt with a zipper and a yoke

Fabric and notions per the pattern envelope (we used a cotton-blend bouclé tweed, matching thread, vintage rickrack, and ¼-inch twill tape)—*remember to buy a longer zipper*

Basic skirt-making tools and materials (page 47)

EASY BEGINNER

Cheat sheet for easy beginner on page 49

Pattern schematics on page 110

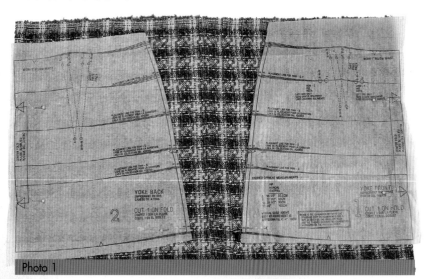

Photo 1

A little more bass in this mix?

4 Stitch the yoke front to the yoke back at the side seams, right sides together, leaving the left side open above the notch. Backstitch at the notch to secure the seam.

5 Cut a piece of rickrack to the width of the yoke at each placement line. (The piece for the top placement line will be shorter, since the yoke is narrower at that point.) Pin each piece of rickrack to its corresponding placement line, having the ends even with the open edges on the left side. Stitch the rickrack in place with a single line of stitching (photo 2).

6 Stitch front to back at the side seams, right sides together, matching the notches. Make two lines of parallel stitching near the bottom of the skirt, one at 1 inch and one at ¾ inch from the edge. Leave the hem otherwise unfinished (photo 3).

7 With right sides together, pin the upper edge of the skirt front and back to the lower edge of the yoke, matching centers, side seams, and notches. Stitch, remembering to remove the pins as you reach them (photo 4). Press the seam open.

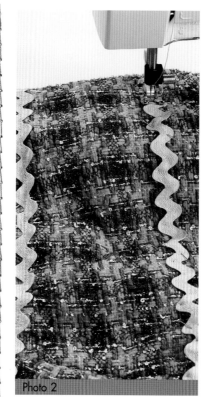

Photo 2

Photo 3

Photo 4

8 To install the zipper on the left side, turn in ½ inch on the back opening edge; press. Turn in the front opening edge along the seamline and press. Place the closed zipper under the back opening edge, placing the zipper stop at the notch and the zipper teeth close to the pressed edge. Pin the end of the zipper tape to the skirt. Using a zipper foot, baste the zipper to the skirt and then stitch close to the edge. Lap the front opening edge over the back opening edge, matching seamlines. Baste and then stitch in place, pivoting below the notch. Trim the excess length from the zipper.

9 Now you'll add a facing to the waistline. Apply fusible interfacing to the facing sections following the manufacturer's directions. Stitch the right side seam of the facing sections, right sides together. Finish the long unnotched edge by stitching ¼ inch from the edge; turn under along the stitching, press, and stitch.

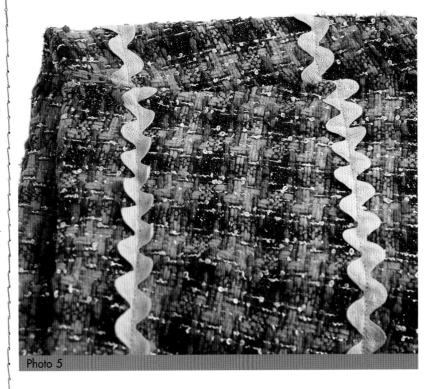

Photo 5

10 With right sides together, pin the facing to the skirt, matching the centers and the right side seams. (The facing extends ½ inch beyond the back opening edge and ⅝ inch beyond the front opening edge.) Baste in place. To prevent stretching, baste a length of twill tape along the seamline. Stitch along the seamline. Trim the seam and clip the curves. (Don't clip the tape.)

11 To understitch the facing, press it away from the skirt, pressing the seam toward the facing. With the facing side up, stitch close to the seam through the facing and the seam allowances.

12 Turn the facing to the inside, turning under and hemstitching the edges to the zipper tape; press. To keep the facing in place, tack it to the seam allowances. Here's the finished, embellished yoke (photo 5).

What a great day
to play!

Gloriously Gathered

This billowy skirt features playful fabric with yards and yards of pretty trim.

WHAT YOU NEED

Pattern for a skirt with a zipper and multiple ruffles

Fabric and notions per the pattern envelope (we used cotton fabric, matching thread, 1-inch vintage trim, and ¼-inch twill tape)— *remember to buy a longer zipper*

Basic skirt-making tools and materials (page 47)

EASY BEGINNER

Cheat sheet for easy beginner on page 49

Pattern schematics on page 110

HOW YOU MAKE IT

1 Cut out and mark the skirt according to your pattern's instructions; we marked three placement lines on the yoke for the trim, one of which is below the zipper. Remember to finish the seam allowances of your skirt, using the method of your choice, and be sure to transfer all of the markings. There's lots of sewing in this skirt, but none of it is difficult. Promise.

2 Staystitch the upper edge of the yoke front ½ inch from the cut edge; be sure to stitch in the direction your pattern indicates. Make the darts in the front and press them toward the center of the skirt.

3 Staystitch the upper edge of the yoke back ½ inch from the cut edge; be sure to stitch in the direction your pattern indicates. Make the darts in the back and press them toward the center of the skirt.

4 Stitch the yoke front to the yoke back at the side seams, right sides together, leaving the left side open above the notch. Backstitch at the notch to secure the seam. (If this is starting to sound familiar, it's because this is pretty much the way the Elegantly Edgy skirt begins, too.)

5 Cut a piece of trim to the width of the yoke at each placement line, adding ¾ inch to the longest piece that will fall below the zipper. (The pieces will vary in length since the yoke is narrower at the top.) Pin the two shorter pieces of trim to

their corresponding placement lines, having the ends even with the open edges on the left side. Pin the longest piece along its placement line below the zipper, turning under the excess to cover the raw end at the side seam. Stitch the trim in place along both edges.

6 Stitch the notched ends of the upper ruffle sections together, right sides facing; these are the side seams. Gather the upper edge by making two parallel rows of basting stitches within the seam allowance, leaving the thread ends long. Pull the thread ends to gather gently (photo 1); you'll adjust the gathers to fit when you stitch the sections together.

7 Stitch the notched ends of the middle ruffle sections together and gather the upper edge, as in step 6.

8 With the right sides together, pin the upper edge of the middle ruffle to the lower edge of the upper ruffle, placing one seam at the center

Photo 1

Photo 2

back of the upper ruffle and the remaining seams at the marked dots on the front of the upper ruffle. Pull up the gathering stitches to fit, distributing the fullness evenly. Baste. When you're working with lots of fabric, it helps to arrange it carefully at the machine before you begin to sew. Stitch; as you accumulate a lot of fabric in front, gently rotate it under the free arm of the machine. Press the seam up. This is how your skirt will look after this step (photo 2).

9 Stitch the notched ends of the lower ruffle sections together and gather the upper edge, as in step 6. Make a narrow hem at the lower edge of this section: Stitch ⅜ inch from the lower edge. Press up the hem along this line of stitching, then tuck under the raw edge to meet the line of stitching. Press. Stitch the hem in place.

10 Fold the lower ruffle in half at one seam and place a pin opposite the seam; this pin will mark the center front and the seam will be the center back. Fold the ruffle in

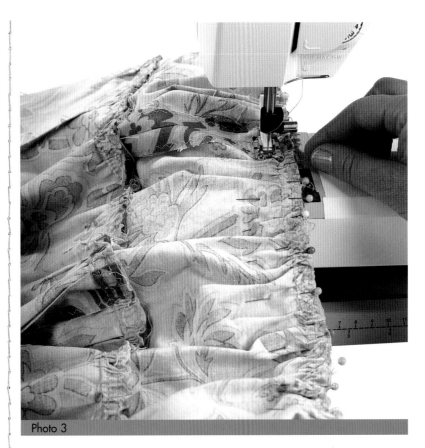

Photo 3

half again and place pins at these folds (you've folded it into quarters now). These pins will mark the side edges. (If you'd like, use a marking tool to mark these four spots.)

11 With the right sides together, pin the upper edge of the lower ruffle to the lower edge of the middle ruffle, placing the seam at the center back and placing the pins (or the marks) at the center front and the side edges of the middle ruffle. Pull up the gathering stitches to fit, distributing the fullness evenly. Baste. Stitch and press the seam up.

12 With the right sides together, pin the upper edge of the ruffle to the lower edge of the yoke, matching the centers and the side seams. Pull up the gathering stitches to fit, distributing the fullness evenly. Baste. Stitch (photo 3) and press the seam toward the yoke.

Photo 4

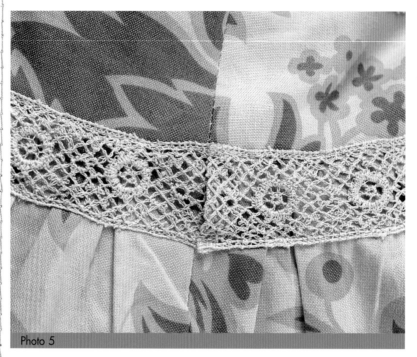

Photo 5

13 Measure and cut pieces of trim to the width of each seam on the skirt, plus ¾ inch. Place the appropriate piece of trim along the yoke seam and pin in place, turning under and lapping one end at the left side seam (photos 4 and 5). Stitch both edges of trim in place. Repeat to add trim to each remaining seam.

14 To install the zipper on the left side, turn in ½ inch on the back opening edge; press. Turn in the front opening edge along the seamline and press. Place the closed zipper under the back opening edge, placing the zipper stop at the notch and the zipper teeth close to the pressed edge. Pin the end of the zipper tape to the skirt. Using a zipper foot, baste the zipper to the skirt and then stitch close to the edge. Lap the front opening edge over the back opening edge, matching seamlines. Baste and then stitch in place, pivoting below the notch. Trim the excess length from the zipper.

15 Now you'll add a facing to the waistline. Apply fusible interfacing to the facing sections following the manufacturer's directions. Stitch the right side seam of the facing sections, right sides together. Finish the long unnotched edge by stitching ¼ inch from the edge; turn under along the stitching, press, and stitch.

16 With right sides together, pin the facing to the skirt, matching the centers and the right side seams. (The facing extends ½ inch beyond the back opening edge and ⅝ inch beyond the front opening edge.) Baste in place. To prevent stretching, baste a length of twill tape along the seamline. Stitch along the seamline. Trim the seam and clip the curves. (Don't clip the tape.)

17 To understitch the facing, press it away from the skirt, pressing the seam toward the facing. With the facing side up, stitch close to the seam through the facing and the seam allowances.

18 Turn the facing to the inside, turning under and hemstitching the edges to the zipper tape; press. To keep the facing in place, tack it to the seam allowances.

Tip

When you're stitching together a very full skirt, arrange it carefully around the free arm of the sewing machine. Stitch until you can't easily manage the bulk of the fabric in front of the machine. Stop stitching, gently pull the skirt under the free arm to the back, and resume stitching.

Lusciously Layered

Delicate fabrics are wonderful in layers, aren't they?

WHAT YOU NEED

Pattern for a bias-cut, layered skirt with a zipper

Fabric and notions per the pattern envelope (we used silk chiffon, matching thread, ⅝-inch ribbon, and silk pins)—*remember to buy a longer zipper*

Basic skirt-making tools and materials (page 47)

EXPERIENCED BEGINNER

Cheat sheet for experienced beginner on page 49

Pattern schematics on page 110

HOW YOU MAKE IT

1 The side seams in the overskirt and the skirt are stitched with French seams. Here's how these delightful seams are made: Begin by stitching the *wrong* sides together in a ¼-inch seam. Remember that you have to trim the seam very short and turn the fabric inside out so the right sides are together. Now, stitch together in a ⅜-inch seam, encasing the raw edge. Photo 1 shows the French seam in progress; if you need a refresher, see page 35.

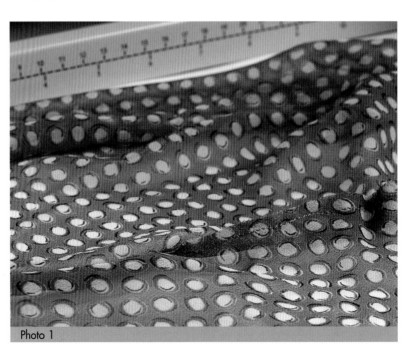

Photo 1

The flowers are lovely. Where's the chocolate?

2 In this pattern, the over-skirt pieces are shorter than the skirt pieces. Begin with the overskirt, where the left side will be left open above the marked circle. Pin the short front and back overskirt sections together at the side seams, clipping to the circle so you can sew the French seams below this point (photo 2). Stitch the French seams. (In photo 3, the first step of the French seam has been completed.) The remaining long front and back sections will be used for the skirt.

3 Make a narrow hem at the lower edge of overskirt, but stitch ⅝ inch from the lower edge instead of ⅜ inch as we've done previously. Press up the hem along this line of stitching, then tuck under the raw edge to meet the line of stitching. Press. Stitch the hem in place; if using chiffon, you may want to sew by hand.

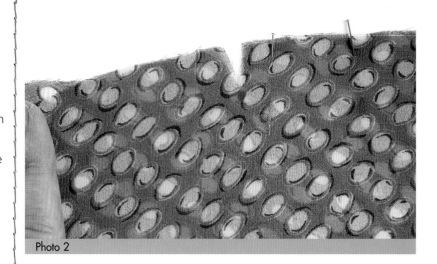

Photo 2

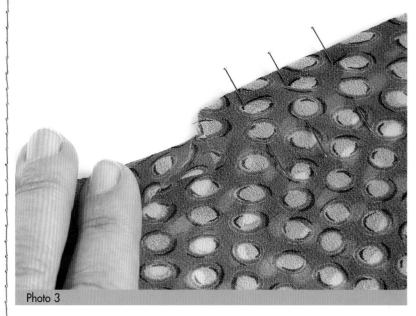

Photo 3

4 To install the zipper on the left side of the overskirt, turn in ½ inch on the back opening edge; press. Turn in the front opening edge along the seamline and press. Place the closed zipper under the back opening edge, placing the zipper stop at the circle and the zipper teeth close to the pressed edge. Pin the end of the zipper tape to the skirt. Using a zipper foot, baste

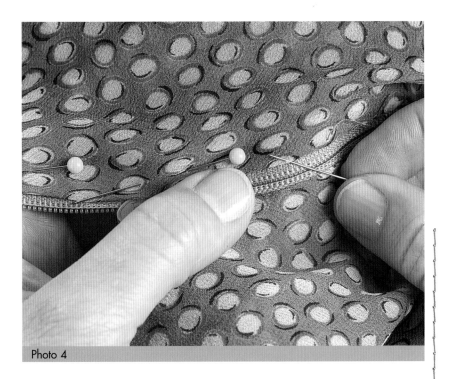

Photo 4

the zipper to the skirt and then stitch close to the edge. Lap the front opening edge over the back opening edge, matching the seamlines. Baste and then stitch in place, pivoting below the circle. Trim the excess length from the zipper.

5 To make the skirt, stitch the front and back sections together with French seams as in step 2, clipping to the marked circle first. Leave the left side open above the circle. Remember to begin with the wrong sides together, okay?

6 Make a ⅜-inch narrow hem at the lower edge of the skirt, using the same method you used in step 3.

7 Pin the right side of the skirt to the wrong side of the overskirt, matching the side seams. Turn under the open edges of the left side of the skirt so they clear the zipper teeth and hemstitch to the zipper tape (photo 4), pinning in place if necessary.

Photo 5

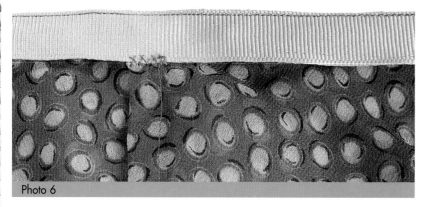

Photo 6

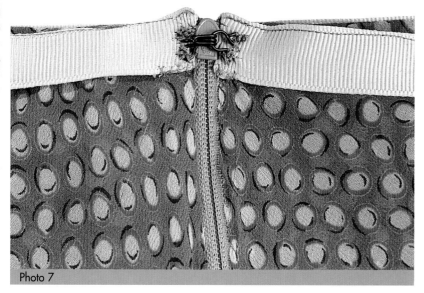

Photo 7

8 Baste together the upper edges of the skirt and the overskirt, leaving the thread ends long.

9 Cut one piece of grosgrain ribbon the length of the waistline guide. Transfer all the markings.

10 On the outside, pin the ribbon to the upper edge of the skirt, placing one long edge along the seamline and matching the small circles to the side seams. Ease the line of basting stitches to fit; baste the ribbon to the skirt (photo 5). Stitch close to the lower edge of the ribbon.

11 Trim the seam allowance close to the stitching, being careful not to cut the ribbon. Turn the ribbon to the inside along the seamline, turning in the ends to clear the zipper teeth. Hemstitch the ribbon ends to the zipper tape. Tack at the seams (photo 6) and tack a hook and eye to the ribbon if desired (photo 7).

Tip

To tempt you, we've included a skirt made from this gorgeous chiffon. But you should use it only after you've gained a bit of sewing experience. Chiffon is all about me, me, me, and it must be treated delicately.

It should be cut out on a non-slippery surface, such as felt, with the pattern pieces held in place with weights designed for that purpose. While sewing, use silk pins; set your machine to a light tension and a shorter-than-normal stitch length. Use the French seam technique for any straight seams.

If you're wary of using chiffon, remember that your pattern envelope will suggest a variety of other fabrics you can use for your skirt.

I think the traffic has stopped!

$\mathcal{S}$ophisticated Simplicity

*Pleats and bows suggest femininity and fun,
yet the tailored lines suit the office, too.*

WHAT YOU NEED

Pattern for a pleated skirt with a zipper and a waistband

Fabric and notions per the pattern envelope (we used cotton fabrics and matching thread)—*remember to buy a longer zipper*

Basic skirt-making tools and materials (page 47)

EXPERIENCED BEGINNER

Cheat sheet for experienced beginner on page 49

Pattern schematics on page 110

HOW YOU MAKE IT

1 Cut out and mark the skirt according to your pattern's instructions. Remember to finish the seam allowances of your skirt, using the method of your choice.

2 To make the pleats in each front and back section, fold the fabric to bring the marked stitching lines and large circles together on the inside. Baste. (We used contrasting thread to baste this skirt.) Stitch along the stitching lines, ending at the marked squares (photo 1). Remove the basting stitches.

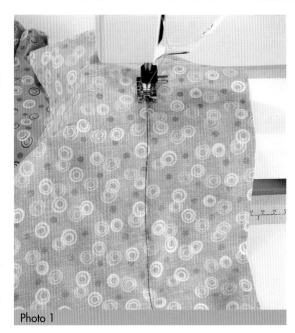

Photo 1

3 Press the pleats flat. Baste them in place across the upper edges (photo 2).

4 Stitch the front to the back at the side seams, right sides together, matching the notches. Leave the left side free above the large marked circle.

5 Easestitch the upper edge of the skirt (photo 3).

6 Now you'll add a waistband. Apply fusible interfacing to one front waistband section and one back waistband section following the manufacturer's directions (the remaining sections will be used as the facing). Stitch the right side seam of the waistband sections, right sides together (photo 4).

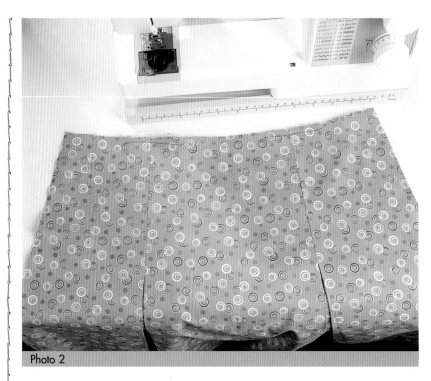

Photo 2

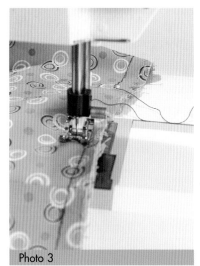

Photo 3

7 Pin the waistband to the upper edge of the skirt, matching notches, centers and right side seams. Adjust the ease. Baste. Stitch and trim the seam allowances, pressing them toward the waistband.

8 To install the zipper on the left side, turn in ½ inch on the back opening edge; press. Turn in the front opening edge along the seamline and press. Place the closed zipper under the back opening edge, placing the zipper stop at the circle and the zipper teeth close to the pressed edge. Pin the end of the zipper tape to the skirt.

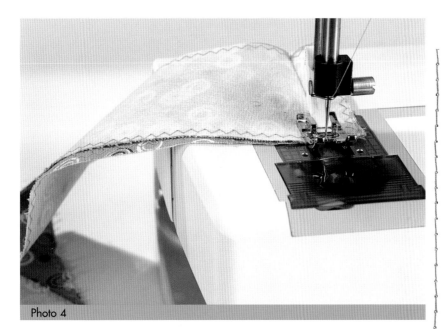

Photo 4

Using a zipper foot, baste the zipper to the skirt and then stitch close to the edge. Lap the front opening edge over the back opening edge, matching seamlines. Baste and then stitch in place, pivoting below the notch. Trim the excess length from the zipper.

9 Stitch the right side seam of the waistband facing sections, right sides together. Press under ⅝ inch on the long notched edge of the waistband facing, easing in fullness. Trim the pressed edge to ⅜ inch.

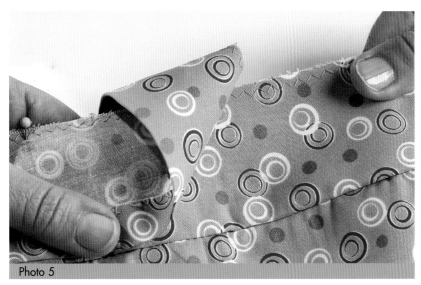

Photo 5

10 Pin the waistband facing to the waistband (photo 5). Stitch along the upper edge. Trim the seam. Press the seam allowances toward the facing. Understitch the facing: Press it away from the skirt, pressing the seam toward the facing. With the facing side up, stitch close to the seam through the facing and the seam allowances.

11 Turn the facing to the inside, turning under and hemstitching the edges to the zipper tape and over the seam.

12 We used complementary fabric to make the bows and a band at the hem. Here's how we made the band: Use the bottom 2 inches of your skirt front and back as a pattern and cut the band. Stitch the band together at the sides as you did the skirt. Make a narrow hem at the bottom of the band (photo 6); stitch it to the skirt bottom with right sides together. Press the seam toward the hem.

13 Make your own fabric bows by cutting two strips of fabric that are each 1 x 20 inches. Fold each bow in half lengthwise. Turn the raw edges into the middle and press. Stitch along the edge (photo 7). Tack each bow in place above a pleat (photo 8).

Photo 6

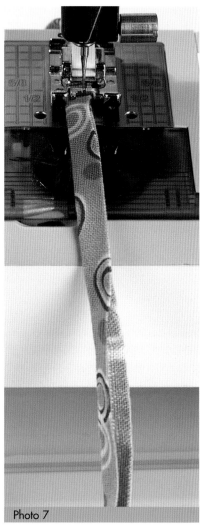

Photo 7

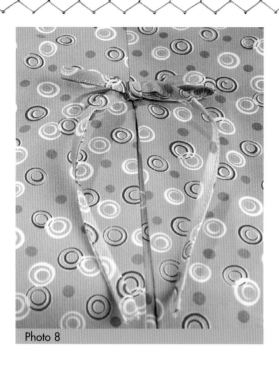

Photo 8

Tip

Have you ever shopped for fabric at quilting stores? They're great resources for finding fabrics in different colorways, such as those we used in this project.

Artfully Arranged

An elegant black skirt with peek-a-boo tulle at the hem is perfect for a stylish celebration.

WHAT YOU NEED

Pattern for a full, lined skirt with a zipper and a yoke

Fabric and notions per the pattern envelope (we used cotton eyelet, cotton lining, matching thread, and matching tulle)—*remember to buy a longer zipper*

Basic skirt-making tools and materials (page 47)

EXPERIENCED

BEGINNER

Cheat sheet for experienced beginner on page 49

Pattern schematics on page 110

HOW YOU MAKE IT

1 Cut out and mark the skirt according to your pattern's instructions. Remember to finish the seam allowances of your skirt, using the method of your choice.

2 Stitch the center back seam in two yoke back sections from the lower edge to the large marked circle, right sides together. (The remaining yoke backs will be used for facings.)

3 To install the zipper in the back of the yoke, turn in ½ inch on the right opening edge; press. Turn in the left opening edge along the seamline and press. Place the closed zipper under the right opening edge, placing the zipper stop at the circle and the zipper teeth close to the pressed edge. Pin the end of the zipper tape to the skirt. Using a zipper foot, baste the zipper to the skirt and then stitch close to the edge; contrasting basting thread is easier

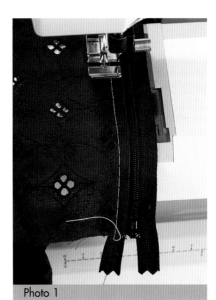

Photo 1

to remove in a dark fabric like this (photo 1). Lap the left opening edge over the right opening edge, matching seamlines. Baste and then stitch in place, pivoting below the notch. Trim the excess length from the zipper.

You're taking my picture, aren't you?

4 Stitch the yoke front to the yoke back at the side seams, right sides together. (The remaining yoke front will be used for the facing.)

5 Stitch the front to the back at the side seams, right sides together, matching the notches. Stitch together the skirt front and skirt back lining sections as you did the skirt.

6 Turn under a 2-inch hem at the lower edge of the lining. Press. Baste close to the fold. Baste ¼ inch from the raw edge and press under. Pull the basting thread at the raw edge and ease to fit (photos 2 and 3). Hem in place by hand. (If you want to know why you're doing this, see the box on page 99.)

7 Stitch the ruffle sections together at the short edges, right sides together. Add a second row of stitching in the seam allowance. Press the seams to one side.

Photo 2

Photo 3

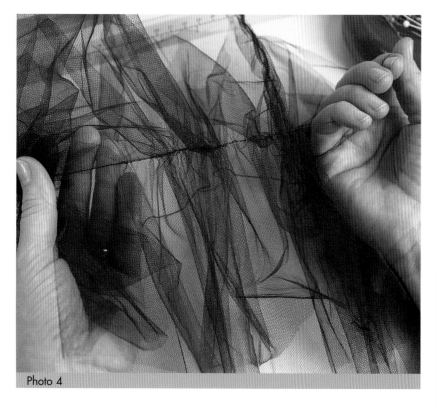

Photo 4

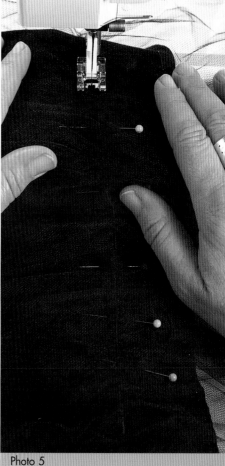

Photo 5

8 Gather the ruffle along the stitching line between the side seams (photo 4). Pin the ruffle to the right side of the lining, placing the line of gathering stitches on the placement line, matching centers and side seams. Adjust the gathers. Stitch along the line of gathering stitches (photo 5). After you've finished stitching, fold the ruffle in half along the line of stitching.

9 Pin the right side of the lining to the wrong side of the skirt at the upper edge, matching notches, centers, and side seams. Baste.

Photo 6

10 Pin the yoke to the skirt, right sides together, matching notches, centers, and side seams, keeping the zipper free. Stitch (photo 6). Clip the seam at the edges of the zipper tape. Trim the seam. Press the seam allowances toward the yoke and press down the end of the zipper.

11 Stitch the yoke back and the yoke front facing sections together at the side seams, right sides together. Press under ⅝ inch at the lower and the back opening edges, folding in the fullness at the corners and easing in the fullness at the lower edge (photo 7).

12 Pin the facing to the yoke at the upper edge, right sides together, matching notches, side seams, and back opening edges. Stitch. Trim the seam allowances. Understitch the facing: Press it away from the skirt, pressing the seam toward the facing. With the facing side up, stitch close to the seam through the facing and the seam allowances.

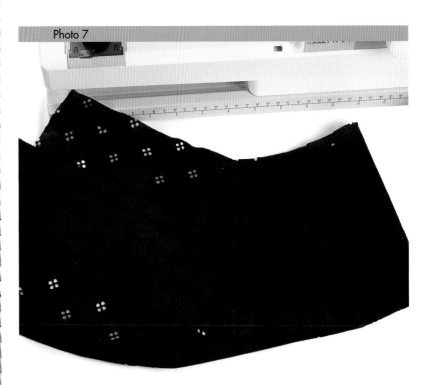

Photo 7

13 Turn the facing to the inside, turning under and slipstitching the edges to the zipper tape and over the seam (photo 8).

14 Turn under a 1¼-inch hem at the lower edge of the skirt. Hem as you did the lining in step 6, easing the hem to fit.

Photo 8

Why

The bottom edge is the widest part of the skirt, so it needs to be eased a teeny bit to fit when it's hemmed. If you turned up a hem without easing it, it would have unsightly folds, so easing allows the hem to lie flat.

Embellishment Techniques

Here's your special bonus section! If you'd like to explore some additional ways to adorn your skirts, try some of these ideas. Here's an overview of some simple embellishment techniques.

Sewing Techniques

Some of the stitches in this section and the embroidery section are interchangeable, as they can be used in dressmaking or embroidery.

APPLIQUÉ. The applying of one fabric layer to another. You can stitch appliqués by machine or by hand, using practically any of the stitches described in this section.

BLANKET STITCH. This loop stitch can be decorative or functional. After anchoring the thread near the fabric edge from the wrong side, insert the needle from the right side so it's perpendicular to the fabric edge. Pass the needle over the thread and pull, repeating for each successive stitch (figure 1).

BUTTONHOLE STITCH. Buttonhole stitch is similar to blanket stitch, but forms a knot at the fabric edge. Working with the needle perpendicular to the fabric edge and the thread behind the needle, loop the thread under the needle and pull (figure 2).

SATIN STITCH. In machine stitching, make a satin stitch with zigzag stitch set to a short length, so the stitches are very close together. For hand stitching, see page 103.

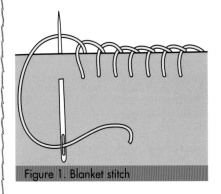

Figure 1. Blanket stitch

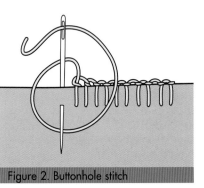

Figure 2. Buttonhole stitch

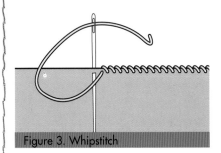

Figure 3. Whipstitch

TOPSTITCH. Machine stitching on the right side of the garment that follows an edge or a seam.

WHIPSTITCH. A utilitarian slanted hand stitch where the needle is inserted perpendicular to the fabric edge (figure 3).

Sequin Techniques

There are several different ways to attach flashy little sequins to your skirts.

WITH A BEAD. If you prefer to hide the thread, add a bead in the center of the sequin. Stitch through the center of the bead from the wrong side, add the bead, and stitch down through the center (figure 4).

Figure 4. Sequin stitching

WITH A DECORATIVE THREAD. If you'd like for the thread to be part of the embellishment, stitch down through the center of the bead, leaving the knot and tail visible (figure 5). As you see here, you can also add a sequin to the underside, should you want the sequins to show on both sides of the fabric—perhaps on a flirty hem?

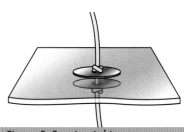
Figure 5. Sequin stitching

IN A LINE. If you'd like to add a line of sequins, use backstitches to secure the sequins (figure 6). This technique is very similar to the beading technique described on page 102.

Figure 6. Sequin stitching

Beading Techniques

Simple bead embroidery can add dazzling highlights to your skirt. To begin, you need only thread, a needle, and, of course, beads. There are specialized threads and needles for beading, but clear nylon thread can work, too. Any fine needle that will pass through the beads can be used as well.

Here are a couple of easy techniques.

SINGLE STITCH. This is basically a running stitch with a bead in each stitch. Each time the needle emerges from the wrong side of the fabric, slide a bead onto it and down to the fabric. Push the needle through to the wrong side just at the edge of the bead (figure 7).

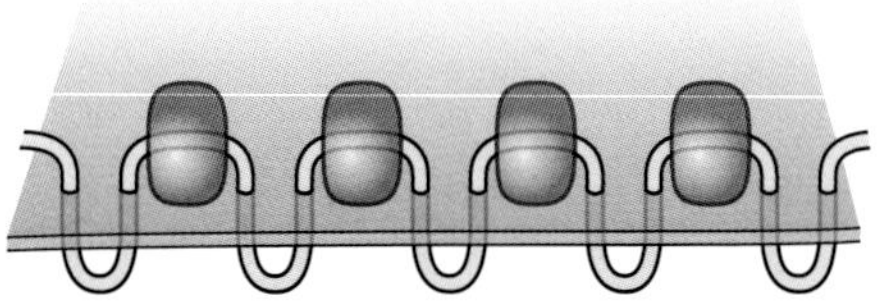

BACKSTITCH. Add an uninterrupted line of beads using the backstitch, attaching either single beads or groups of beads. This stitch is similar to backstitch in regular sewing, with a bead added. Slide a bead onto the needle each time it emerges from the fabric and insert the needle at the edge of the previous bead. Begin the next stitch one bead's length away (figure 8).

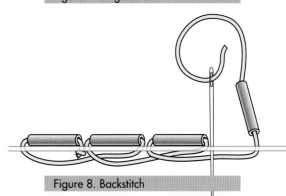

Figure 7. Single stitch

Figure 8. Backstitch

Embroidery Techniques

Embroidery is an age-old embellishment technique. The tools and supplies you need for hand embroidery are few: floss, needles, an embroidery hoop, and perhaps a marking tool or quilter's tape. Usually, you'll want to separate the floss so you're working with three or fewer strands. Carefully place your skirt into an embroidery hoop for stability, if possible, and mark the placement of your stitches, if necessary.

Here are some basic embroidery stitches.

RUNNING STITCH. An easy stitch to execute, the running stitch is simply made by weaving the needle through the garment at evenly spaced intervals (figure 9).

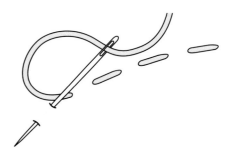

Figure 9. Running stitch

STRAIGHT STITCH. Use a series of straight stitches used to create a motif (figure 10).

SATIN STITCH. Satin stitch is composed of parallel rows of straight stitches (figure 11).

CROSS-STITCH. Cross-stitch is a series of diagonal stitches. The finished stitches can be touching one another or separated by space, as desired (figure 12).

FRENCH KNOTS. The elegant French knot is created by wrapping the thread around the needle once or twice (or thrice!), then inserting it back into the garment at the point where the needle emerged (figure 13).

WOVEN WHEELS. This fanciful stitch can be varied to be as full as desired. Begin by making an odd number of straight stitches and covering them with floss, alternately going over one stitch and under the next. You can completely cover the stitches, if desired (figure 14).

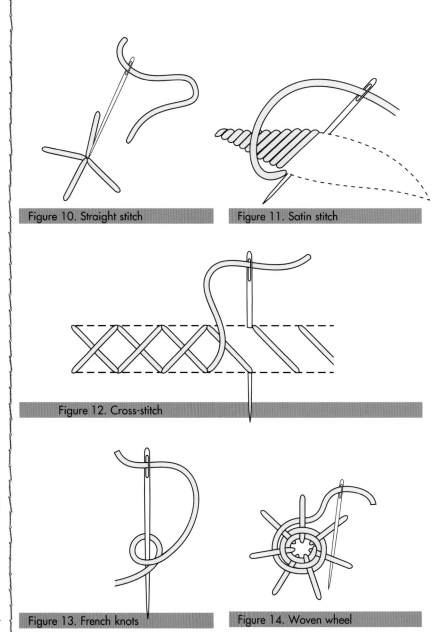

Figure 10. Straight stitch

Figure 11. Satin stitch

Figure 12. Cross-stitch

Figure 13. French knots

Figure 14. Woven wheel

Glossary

BACKSTITCH. A stitch worked from left to right; each new stitch ends at the left side of the previous stitch.

BASTING STITCH. A long, straight stitch used to hold pieces together temporarily or to gather.

BIAS. The diagonal between the lengthwise and crosswise threads in woven fabric. Fabric has the most stretch in this direction.

CASING. A channel of fabric created to contain elastic or cording.

DART. A construction technique to create shape and fit in a garment.

EASE. This term has two different meanings. In sewing, ease means to adjust the length of one piece to fit another; ease-stitching with basting stitches is used when joining two pieces that are slightly unequal in length. In fashion, ease is the amount of sizing added to patterns to allow movement or for design purposes.

EASESTITCHING. See *ease*.

FACING. A separate piece of fabric used to finish an edge; in this book, the waistline of a skirt is often finished with a facing.

FLOUNCE. A circular ruffle that isn't gathered to fit.

FREE ARM. A narrow sewing surface created when a removable accessory tray is detached from the sewing machine.

GRAIN. The direction of the threads in woven fabric.

HEMSTITCH. A hand stitch that catches a thread of the garment and a thread of a folded edge.

INTERFACING. A special fabric that's used to stabilize parts of a garment.

MUSLIN. A copy of the garment with major seams sewn together. A muslin is designed to test fit.

NOTIONS. All the other items you need to sew in addition to the pattern and the fabric.

PIVOT. To turn the fabric to change direction while sewing. Pivot by stopping with the needle in the fabric, lifting the presser foot, and turning the fabric.

PRESS. To move the iron across the fabric by pressing it up and down, as opposed to sliding it.

SEAM ALLOWANCE. This is the amount of space between the edge of the fabric and the seamline. In garment sewing, ⅝ inch is the standard seam allowance.

SEAMLINE. The stitching line.

SELVAGE. The finished border on a length of fabric.

STAYSTITCHING. A line of stitching sewn ½ inch into the seam allowance to stabilize the piece.

STRAIGHT STITCH. The basic sewing machine stitch.

TACK. A straight stitch to join interior layers of fabric, such as a facing to a seam allowance.

UNDERSTITCHING. A line of stitching close to a seam that's designed to keep a piece in place. Facings are often understitched, for example.

YOKE. A portion of a skirt made to fit the waist and hips.

ZIGZAG. A machine stitch in which the needle moves from side to side as it sews.

Metric Conversion Chart

INCHES	MILLIMETERS (MM)/ CENTIMETERS (CM)	INCHES	MILLIMETERS (MM)/ CENTIMETERS (CM)
⅛	3 mm	15½	39.4 cm
³⁄₁₆	5 mm	16	40.6 cm
¼	6 mm	16½	41.9 cm
⁵⁄₁₆	8 mm	17	43.2 cm
⅜	9.5 mm	17½	44.5 cm
⁷⁄₁₆	1.1 cm	18 (½ yard)	45.7 cm
½	1.3 cm	18½	47 cm
⁹⁄₁₆	1.4 cm	19	48.3 cm
⅝	1.6 cm	19½	49.5 cm
¹¹⁄₁₆	1.7 cm	20	50.8 cm
¾	1.9 cm	20½	52 cm
¹³⁄₁₆	2.1 cm	21	53.3
⅞	2.2 cm	21½	54.6
¹⁵⁄₁₆	2.4 cm	22	55 cm
1	2.5 cm	22½	57.2 cm
1½	3.8 cm	23	58.4 cm
2	5 cm	23½	59.7 cm
2½	6.4 cm	24	61 cm
3	7.6 cm	24½	62.2 cm
3½	8.9 cm	25	63.5 cm
4	10.2 cm	25½	64.8 cm
4½	11.4 cm	26	66 cm
5	12.7 cm	26½	67.3 cm
5½	14 cm	27	68.6 cm
6	15.2 cm	27½	69.9 cm
6½	16.5 cm	28	71.1 cm
7	17.8 cm	28½	72.4 cm
7½	19 cm	29	73.7 cm
8	20.3 cm	29½	74.9 cm
8½	21.6 cm	30	76.2 cm
9 (¼ yard)	22.9 cm	30½	77.5 cm
9½	24.1 cm	31	78.7 cm
10	25.4 cm	31½	80 cm
10½	26.7 cm	32	81.3 cm
11	27.9 cm	32½	82.6 cm
11½	29.2 cm	33	83.8 cm
12	30.5 cm	33½	85 cm
12½	31.8 cm	34	86.4 cm
13	33 cm	34½	87.6 cm
13½	34.3 cm	35	88.9 cm
14	35.6 cm	35½	90.2 cm
14½	36.8 cm	36 (1 yard)	91.4 cm
15	38.1 cm		

Designer Biographies

The artistic endeavors of *Joan K. Morris* have led her down many successful creative paths, including ceramics and costume design for motion pictures. Joan has contributed projects for numerous Lark books, including *Beautiful Ribbon Crafts* (2003), *Halloween: A Grown-up's Guide to Creative Costumes* (2003), *Hardware Style* (2003), *The Michaels Book of Wedding Crafts* (2005), and *Hip Handbags* (2005). Joan's skirts are on pages 52, 56, 82, and 94.

Nathalie Mornu has made projects for many Lark books, including *Decorating Your First Apartment* (2002), *The Weekend Crafter: Making Gingerbread Houses* (2004), and *Hip Handbags* (2005). She lives in Asheville, North Carolina, but looks for shiny things wherever she may be. See Nathalie's skirts on pages 72, 76, and 88.

Acknowledgments

I'm so relieved that sewing is cool again. I haven't been this hip in a long time.

Stylish Skirts gave me an opportunity to explore some of the contemporary techniques I'd seen in boutiques and catalogs for the last few years. Although I've been sewing for quite some time (I'd rather not say how long, if it's all the same to you), using fresh ideas was like learning to sew all over again. I hope I conveyed my real enthusiasm for sewing to you, the beginner, in this book focusing solely on skirts. The skirt is a timeless garment that can be continually reinvented, so go for it! Take these ideas and run with them. Knowledge is power and creativity is power*ful*.

A talented group of people helped bring this book to life. I'm grateful for the skill and good humor of the gifted sewers who helped me make the skirts, Joan Morris and Nathalie Mornu. (Humor is vitally important when you make a book. Especially one that involves needles and sewing machines.) Photographer Stewart O'Shields and his assistant, Effie Paroutsas, created wonderful visuals, and Art Director Susan McBride designed and illustrated a beautiful book (as usual). Associate Editor Nathalie Mornu (yep, her again) and Assistant Editor Rebecca Guthrie were indispensable to the production of the book.

My sincere thanks to The McCall Pattern Company and the Simplicity Pattern Co. Inc., for permission to use their designs in this book. Without their gracious cooperation this project wouldn't have happened.

Several businesses in Asheville, North Carolina, let us disrupt their operations so we could use their establishments or wares for our photo shoots. Sincere thanks to the following: The Bier Garden; Bobo's; Rags Reborn; Salsa's; and Asheville Scooter. Artist Lauren Gibbes graciously allowed us into her studio; Terry and Steve Moberg graciously allowed us into their condo; and Susan McBride and Michael Murphy graciously allowed us into their backyard.

You've probably already guessed that I come from a long line of seamstresses and DIYers. Long before the term was fashionable, my mother was taking things apart and attempting to put them back together again. She also sat me down at the sewing machine and taught me to sew. Inspired by Mom and both my grandmothers, I churned out my entire wardrobe in high school—jumpers to bellbottoms, cheerleading outfits to prom dresses, jackets to halter tops, and everything in between. So I'd like to dedicate this series of sewing books to my mother, Doris Van Arsdale, for letting me make short skirts and hot pants—and then allowing me to actually wear them.

BTW, I did make that pair of pink culottes referenced in the introduction. It was the first garment I ever made (thanks again, Mom), and they were actually cute. Really!

Pattern Credits

The patterns used on pages 56, 82, 88, and 94 are courtesy of The McCall Pattern Company, 11 Penn Plaza, New York, New York 11215.

The patterns used on pages 52, 60, 64, 68, 72, and 76 are courtesy of Simplicity Pattern Co. Inc. 2 Park Avenue, 12th Floor, New York, New York 10016.

A Note About Suppliers

Usually, the supplies you need for making the projects in Lark books can be found at your local craft supply store, discount mart, home improvement center, or retail shop relevant to the topic of the book. Occasionally, however, you may need to buy materials or tools from specialty suppliers. In order to provide you with the most up-to-date information, we have created a list of suppliers on our website, which we update on a regular basis. Visit us at www.larkbooks.com, click on "Craft Supply Sources," and then click on the relevant topic. You will find numerous companies listed with their web address and/or mailing address and phone number.

Pattern Schematics

To give you some perspective on the patterns we used, here are drawings of the pieces in each design.

POLKA DOT PERFECTION
1. Front and Back

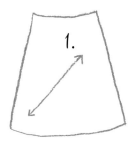

SIMPLY STYLISH
1. Front and Back
2. Lower Front and Back Band
3. Drawstring

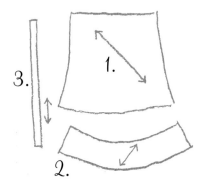

FLIRTY FLOUNCE
1. Back
2. Front
3. Back Facing
4. Front Facing
5. Front and Back Flounce

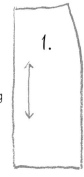

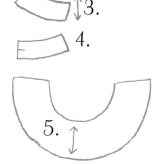

EASILY EMBELLISHED
1. Front
2. Side Front
3. Back
4. Side Back
5. Front Facing
6. Back Facing

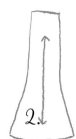

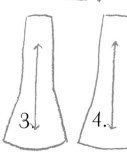

INTENTIONALLY ASYMMETRICAL
1. Upper Front and Back
2. Middle Front and Back
3. Lower Front and Back
4. Front and Back Facing

ELEGANTLY EDGY

1. Yoke Front
2. Yoke Back
3. Front Facing
4. Back Facing
5. Front and Back

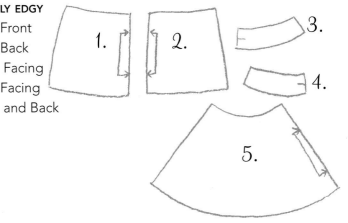

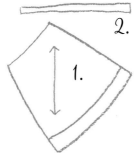

LUSCIOUSLY LAYERED

1. Front and Back (Skirt and Overskirt)
2. Waistline Guide

GLORIOUSLY GATHERED

1. Yoke Front   5. Upper Ruffle
2. Yoke Back   6. Middle Ruffle
3. Front Facing   7. Lower Ruffle
4. Back Facing

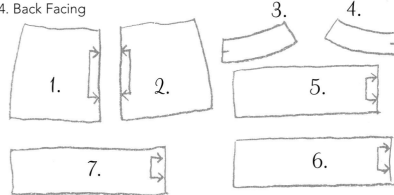

SOPHISTICATED SIMPLICITY

1. Front and Back
2. Front Waistband
3. Back Waistband

ARTFULLY ARRANGED

1. Yoke Back
2. Yoke Front
3. Front and Back
4. Ruffle

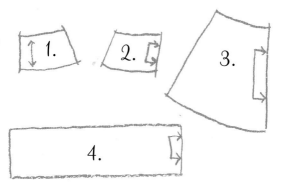

Index